The Risk of Education

T0158454

The Risk of Education
Discovering Our Ultimate Destiny

LUIGI GIUSSANI

TRANSLATED BY MARIANGELA SULLIVAN

McGill-Queen's University Press
Montreal & Kingston • London • Chicago

ISBN 978-0-7735-5749-9 (cloth)
ISBN 978-0-7735-5718-5 (paper)
ISBN 978-0-7735-5719-2 (ePDF)
ISBN 978-0-7735-5720-8 (ePUB)

Legal deposit first quarter 2019
Bibliothèque nationale du Québec

Reprinted 2024

Printed in Canada on acid-free paper that is 100% ancient forest free
(100% post-consumer recycled), processed chlorine free

We acknowledge the support of the Canada Council for the Arts.
Nous remercions le Conseil des arts du Canada de son soutien.

McGill-Queen's University Press in Montreal is on land which long served
as a site of meeting and exchange amongst Indigenous Peoples, including the
Haudenosaunee and Anishinabeg nations. In Kingston it is situated on the
territory of the Haudenosaunee and Anishinaabek. We acknowledge and thank
the diverse Indigenous Peoples whose footsteps have marked these territories
on which peoples of the world now gather.

Library and Archives Canada Cataloguing in Publication

Giussani, Luigi
[Rischio educativo. English]
The risk of education : discovering our ultimate destiny / Luigi Giussani.

Translation of: Il rischio educativo.
Includes bibliographical references.
Issued in print and electronic formats.
ISBN 978-0-7735-5749-9 (hardcover). – ISBN 978-0-7735-5718-5 (paper). –
ISBN 978-0-7735-5719-2 (ePDF). – ISBN 978-0-7735-5720-8 (ePUB)

1. Education – Aims and objectives. I. Title. II. Title: Il rischio educativo. English.

LB41.G5313 2018   370.11   c2018-905710-6
                                         c2018-905711-4

Contents

Foreword

Stanley Hauerwas

I find myself in an extremely embarrassing position. At least it is an extremely embarrassing position for me. I am one of those people who thinks it is better to have views than arguments. I suppose that a view is a kind of argument, if you believe as I do that arguments depend on judgments that, if they are really judgments, are not arbitrary. So, I seldom find myself without anything to say. Indeed, most people think I have had far too much to say because I am far too willing to pronounce on almost anything. My weakness is that there is almost nothing in which I am not interested. My strength is that there is almost nothing in which I am not interested.

I am, moreover, not only interested in education but, in particular, the kind of innovative suggestions Monsignor Luigi Giussani makes for reclaiming education as a Christian activity. I thought I would, therefore, have much to say about Giussani's book *The Risk of Education*. But alas, I find myself in such fundamental agreement with him that it seems all I can do is say, "I wish I had said that."

In truth, I have said some of what Giussani has said in his book. I think much of my criticism of contemporary universities is quite similar to Giussani's critique of secular educational practices in secondary schools.[1] So I fear what follows is no more than my attempt to show how some of my concerns about the kind of education students receive in the colleges and universities of America confirm Giussani's critique of secular education.[2]

One of the reasons I find myself in sympathy with Giussani's work is that my reflections about education and, in particular, the education represented in the modern university have always been part of my project to reclaim the significance of the virtues for any account of the moral life. A focus on the virtues means you cannot easily separate what you come to know from how you come to know. Any knowledge worth having cannot help but shape who we are and accordingly our understanding of the world. Thus I use the description *moral formation*, rather than *education*, because I think all education, whether acknowledged or not, is moral formation.

This is particularly true in courses that are *not* officially thought of as "ethics." For example, consider the moral seriousness of medical education in comparison to the training seminarians receive today. Students in seminaries too often think it more important for them to take courses in counselling (after all, that is how you help people) rather than to take courses in

Christology. In medical school, however, no student gets to decide whether she or he will or will not take anatomy. If you are going to be a doctor, you will take anatomy or give up your ambition to be one. Anatomy may not sound like a course in ethics, but the kind of work young physicians are required to do if they are to study anatomy, I think, is rightly described as moral formation.

The intellectual and moral seriousness of medical education compared to seminary education can be attributed to a set of cultural presuppositions that are crucial for how we understand the training of students for medicine and for the ministry. Quite simply, no one believes in our day that an inadequately trained priest might damage their salvation; but people do believe an inadequately trained doctor can hurt them. Thus, people are much more concerned about who their doctor may be than who is their priest. That such is the case, of course, indicates that no matter how seriously we may think of ourselves as Christians, we may well be living lives that betray our conviction that God matters.

In his book *The Restructuring of American Religion*, Robert Wuthnow observes that one of the trends in church life in America in the second half of the last century was the increasing growth of the laity who had college educations. He notes it was extremely rare in the 1950s for Baptist, Lutheran, or Catholic churches to have more than one in seven who had gone to college. Methodists and Presbyterians might have had a ratio of one to four. By the 1970s, at least one person in four had been to college in most denominations, and in several, the college-educated were a clear majority. He suggests these "proportions would likely have been even larger had it not been for the fact that college-educated people fled the churches in droves in the 1960s."[3] It seems, at least if Wuthnow's study is correct, that the single best indicator of whether as a person ages they will be identified with a church is determined by their having gone to a college or a university.[4]

There are many reasons that may account for this development. The social unrest of the 1960s associated with Vietnam or the change in sexual practices during the same period may have created the conditions that led many to think the church was irrelevant to their lives. No doubt the relation between college education and the increased earning power of those who have achieved it had and continues to have an effect if you believe – as I believe we are required to by the Gospel – that being wealthy is a disability for anyone who desires to be a Christian. I am sure no one factor is sufficient to account for the loss of membership in the mainline Protestant Churches in America.

That said, however, I think it would be a mistake not to take seriously that what many learned, or thought they learned, in colleges and universities led them to abandon Christianity. That students took course after course in which there was no discernible connection to Christian claims about the way things are surely created made the conditions that led to the conclusion that Christianity is at best irrelevant, and at worst false, hard to avoid. In other words, I suspect that many people who leave their Christianity behind after they have gone to college do so because they have been created by God to desire the truth. Yet that desire has been formed by knowledge that seems to make it impossible for them to think that what Christians believe could be true. At best they assume the church may be important for spiritual or moral issues, but those spheres of life are not considered to be about truth.

The strategies of many Christian colleges and universities, both Catholic and Protestant, unfortunately served to underwrite the presumption that the "Christian" part of education did not have to do with "truth." What made a school "Christian" was not the content of the courses but a concern for the "whole student." Student life, therefore, became the locus for any expression of Christianity. The relegation of strong religious beliefs to the "personal" side of life in modern universities reflected the distinction between the private and the public imposed on the church by liberal political regimes. Christian theologians aided this development by underwriting what Douglas Sloan identifies as a two-realm theory of truth.[5] Such a view distinguished the truths of science – which are thought to be objective and impersonal – from the truths of faith, which are then called subjective, grounded as they are in feelings, convention, or "common human experience."

These attempts to forge a "peace treaty" between the Christian faith and what was assumed to be more objective modes of knowledge are increasingly being called into question. Unfortunately, the critics that are challenging the forms of knowledge that so dominate the contemporary university are not drawing on the resources of Christian theology. As a matter of fact, the challenges too often seem to make problematic whether we can know anything at all. The critics of modernity frequently only underwrite the fragmentation of the university curricula. As a result, Alasdair MacIntyre observes:

> What the Catholic faith confronts today in American higher education and indeed in American education more generally is not primarily some range of alternative beliefs about the order of things, but rather a belief that there is no such thing as the order of things of which there could be a unified, if complex, understanding or even a movement toward such an understanding. There is on this contemporary view nothing to understanding except what is supplied by the specialized and professionalized disciplines and subdisciplines. Higher education has become a set of assorted and heterogeneous specialized enquiries into a set of assorted and heterogeneous subject-matters, and general education is a set of introductions to these enquiries together with a teaching of the basic skills necessary for initiation into them, something to be got through in order to advance beyond it into the specialized disciplines.[6]

MacIntyre makes clear he is not against specialization – because any discipline, even philosophy, cannot do its work well without detailed investigations. Yet in modern university curricula, every course threatens to be an introductory course, because the faculties even in their disciplines cannot agree on what needs to be learned first to make later learning possible. As a result, every course a student takes has to begin with a beginning that from the student's perspective is constantly changing. This is particularly true in the humanities; but given the increasing specialized character of the individual sciences, these are beginning to suffer the same fate as well.

From MacIntyre's perspective, the fragmentation of the curriculum makes it all the more important that Catholic universities recognize the significance of philosophy for any serious education that has any pretense of inculcating in students the skills necessary for those who would love the truth. According to MacIntyre, philosophy is the discipline committed to the inquiry necessary to understand how the disciplines that make up the university contribute to, but cannot themselves supply, an understanding of the order of things.[7] So a Catholic university cannot be such if it does not require students to study philosophy not only at the beginning of their study but also at the end.

Yet of equal importance, according to MacIntyre, is the study of theology. Catholic teaching rightly maintains that the natural order of things cannot be adequately understood by reason if reason is divorced from the recognition that all that is has been brought into being by God and is directed to the ends to which God orders creation. What is learned from nature about God, MacIntyre notes, will always be meagre as well as subject to the human limitations and distortions resulting from our sinfulness. Yet it remains the case that "universities always need both the enlargement of vision and the correction of error that can be provided only from a theological stand-point, one that brings truths of Christian revelation to bear on our studies."[8]

I am fundamentally in agreement with MacIntyre's account of the challenges facing us if we are to think seriously about what it means to reclaim education as a Christian enterprise. So I have nothing but sympathy for Giussani's attempt to help us see why and how Christians must reclaim education as a task of the church.

The story he tells in the introduction to the 1995 edition of *The Risk of Education*, about his first confrontation with students who did not believe matters of faith had anything to do with reason, is a wonderful example of why education matters and why it matters for moral formation (p. XXXVI).[9] I think Giussani, moreover, is right to insist that faith is "the supreme rationality" (p. XL). But to so argue means you have to confront, as Giussani did, the deceits of modernity represented by people like Professor Miccinesi; that is, the teachers of the students who think faith has nothing to do with truth or this world.[10] I fear Professor Miccinesi, moreover, is a prime example of the challenge Christians face in education today. The problem quite simply is that the secular have become so stupid that they do not even recognize they do not and, indeed, cannot understand the commonplaces that make the Christian faith the Christian faith.

So I find myself in profound sympathy not only with the general argument about education Giussani makes, but also with the finer-grained arguments he uses to sustain his overall perspective. That may seem strange because I am a Protestant; that is, a representative of that form of Christianity that according to Giussani separates "faith from following."[11] Yet unfortunately, I fear Giussani's characterization of Protestantism, at least the Protestantism that now exists, is correct. Put differently: Protestantism now names that form of Christianity that in the name of reform tried to separate the "essentials" of the Christian faith from the contingent. The result was to turn Christianity into a belief system available to the individual without mediation by the church. As a consequence of this separation, Protestants found themselves in modernity without resources to shape a way of life that can resist the forces that threaten to destroy any robust account of Christian "following" necessary for the education of young people as Christians. I fear this is particularly true of the most Protestant country yet founded; that is, the United States of America.

The Materiality of the Faith and the Difference It Makes in Education

The comments made in this last paragraph, however, bring me to the most important challenge Giussani presents for those of us committed to education as moral formation in America. Giussani sees quite well that education is not possible if you restrict education to the classroom. This is particularly true if we are to sustain Christian education. Giussani puts it this way:

> The Christian fact is permanent throughout history. It has a structure that nothing can change because it is a definitive event. Nevertheless, the Christian who lives out this event, in dealing with the cultural, social, and political conditions of his times – unless he lacks intelligence or is totally slothful – cannot help but judge the prevailing ideas and structures from the point of view of his lived faith. As a result, the desire to create an alternative culture and alternative structures is unavoidable.[12]

Though I am often accused of being a fideistic, sectarian tribalist, I think Giussani is exactly right that the Christian faith requires expression in the everyday habits of life.[13] This, of course, is but the outworking of Giussani's claim above that faith requires a "following"; that is, the "recognition of Christ, our love for him shaped by the parameters of time and space in which his event reaches us."[14] Moreover, Giussani's insistence that faith is the highest form of rationality is a correlative of his claim that the Christian faith must be embodied in the practices of a community that will inexorably find itself in tension with the world.

I am aware that I may seem to be making Giussani's viewpoints sound very much like some of the arguments I have made about the necessity of the church to distance itself from the world in which we now find ourselves. But I trust those who know Giussani better than I do will correct me if they think I have misunderstood him. Yet I think my agreement with Giussani provides me with the means to say why I think some have so misunderstood the kind of claims I have been making about why it is so important that the church not accept in liberal societies its relegation into the world of "spiritual." I fear my anti-Constantinianism has led some to think that I have tried to convince Christians to give up on the world by becoming "pure." Nothing could be further from the truth. The church that must exist, if the kinds of arguments I have tried to develop are to be intelligible, must be what Giussani says it must be; that is, a material reality shaping the equally material realities of politics, recreation, art, buying and selling, "personal" relations – in short, the whole of our lives.

I think this has particular importance for how we think about education. If, as Giussani claims, to educate means to help the human soul enter into the totality of the real, then the content of what is taught by Christians may appear quite different from secular subjects. MacIntyre rightly argues that what students have to learn from the standpoint of a Catholic university is that education in physics, history, or economics is incomplete "until it is to some degree illuminated by philosophical enquiry, and all education, including their philosophical education, is incomplete until it is illuminated by theologically grounded insight."[15] Yet I think Giussani is suggesting an even stronger case than that made by MacIntyre. For if Giussani is right about the fact of faith requiring an alternative culture, then it is at least possible that the very content of physics, history, or economics shaped by such a faith may be different.[16]

I need to be very clear about what I am saying about how the practices that comprise the Christian faith may shape the material conditions that make what Christians mean by physics quite different from what physics might mean if it is produced by those who do not share our faith. Am I really suggesting that there might be something like a "Christian physics" or a "Christian economics"? I can only say, "It depends on the character of what is meant by physics or economics in the societies in which the church finds herself." Christians can never fear what we have to learn from honest investigation of the world, even if such investigations are undertaken by those who have no identification as Christians.[17] Yet neither can Christians assume that knowledge of the world is a "given" to be uncritically accepted by them.

For example, if you believe, as MacIntyre and I do, that usury is a practice that Christians must avoid, then how the knowledge called economics is understood may well be different from the understanding of those who do not share our views about usury. Or if you think that force can only be justified on just war grounds, then how you understand the relations between states may be very different from the assumptions of those that assume some form of a balance of power model is necessary for pursuing those research agendas called international relations. Or if you believe, as Christians do, that creation is a more fundamental notion than nature, that may well make a difference in the kind of distinction you think necessary between the study of botany and biology. Surely, for Christians who believe all that is created has purpose, the attempt to understand life mechanistically must be questioned.

MacIntyre is quite right to stress the significance of helping students acquire the intellectual skills necessary to see the interconnection between subjects, but I am suggesting that the very content of what is taught cannot be avoided if Christians are to take the "risk of education." The problem I think is that Christians in modernity have not been what Giussani says we must be; that is, people who create alternative cultures and structures. As a result, we have taught forms of knowledge in Christian schools that cannot help but undermine how Christians should understand the world in which we find ourselves.

For example, consider the implications of Giussani's almost throwaway observation "Fortunately for us, time exists, which makes us grow old" (p. 51) for how medicine, and the sciences that serve medicine, should be understood. I think there is no denying that the current enthusiasm for "genomics" (that branch of science which allegedly will make it possible to "treat" people before they become sick) draws on an extraordinary fear of suffering and death incompatible with Giussani's observation that *luckily* time makes us grow old. Our culture seems increasingly moving to the view that aging itself is an illness, and if it is possible, we ought to create and fund research that promises us that we may be able to get out of life alive. I find it hard to believe that such a science could be supported by a people who begin Lent by being told that we are dust and it is to dust we will return.

For Christians to create an alternative culture and alternative structures to the knowledge produced and taught in universities that are shaped by the fear of death, I think, is a challenge we cannot avoid. Moreover, to educate our children in such an alternative culture will mean that our children cannot presuppose that the education they receive will make it possible for them to be successful actors in a world shaped by an entirely different culture. For Christians to educate our children for the world in which we now find ourselves means providing them with education that will put them at risk. But at least they will have some chance to resist the lies that are assumed to be true because they are taught in university classrooms.

The Culture of Democracy and the Culture of the Church

As I suggested above, some may think I am over-reading Giussani's suggestion that Christians should try to create an alternative culture and structure that shapes how we educate. Some may well think I have made Giussani sound as if he is advocating a more radical position than he in fact is. However, in my defence, I want to end by calling attention to Giussani's remarks on democracy. His discussion of democracy is part of his argument that education is impossible without the recognition of the other. Such a recognition, he suggests, makes possible the dialogue necessary for me to come to a better understanding of who I am. But it is equally true that dialogue is impossible if we enter into it without having some self-knowledge (p. 78). We simply cannot begin any serious dialogue if we think we must start by compromising our convictions in order to reach a common understanding.

Democracy is often defended as that form of social and political life that makes dialogue not only possible but necessary. Yet Giussani argues that the relativism that the "prevailing mentality" so identifies with democracy makes dialogue impossible. He even reports that a "well-known university professor" dared to say to a select audience in Milan that "Catholics, for the very fact that they are Catholic, cannot be citizens of a democratic state. Catholics claim to know the truth, the absolute. It is, therefore, impossible to have a dialogue with them, and, therefore, also impossible to co-exist democratically with them" (p. 80).

Giussani does not say if he agrees with this judgment, but he clearly thinks that the values and practices often identified as democratic are in tension with the culture he thinks necessary to sustain Christian education. Giussani has little use for the "values" taught in the name of sustaining a democratic ethos.[18] Indeed the very language of values – that is, the assumption that the moral life consists in subjective desires – is an indication that the language of economics has subverted serious moral judgments.

For example, Giussani rightly calls into question any education that is based on the assumption that a person has total autonomy. He clearly does not think that we ought to teach in a manner that allows students to make up their own minds. To attempt such an education, as he puts it, only leaves the teenager at the mercy of his likes and dislikes, his instincts, deprived of any standard of development (see p. 32). Giussani observes that an education that assumes the autonomy of the student cannot help but be one based on fear of confrontation with the world and as a result produce people incapable of dealing with a world gone mad.

The rationalism that underwrites assumptions of autonomy "forgets and denies the basic dependency of the self. It forgets or denies the great, original surprise that is evidence" (p. 48).[19] Ironically, the rationalism often defended as necessary for the sustaining of democratic societies can have the opposite effect. Rather than educating students with the openness required for ongoing inquiry, it makes students feel unprepared to know how to go on because they can see no connection between their previous education and more advanced subjects. Skepticism is the result, creating people who believe that the life choices they must make are arbitrary.

Ironically, such a people are incapable of sustaining democracy because as Giussani observes,

> Skepticism is a basic mindset that endures, and the way people move beyond it in practice is by crossing into fanaticism. That is, they cross over into the uncompromising affirmation of one-sidedness. This same situation applies to students who keep their previous religious and moral views even after their unprepared passage through this violent conflict. This is because, to avoid giving up their views, they cling to them, practically barricading themselves into a fortress of prudence or of fear, which, in any case, is totally without openness toward what they consider to be a hostile environment. Other young people, equally unprepared for the clash, react by turning their backs in an uncritical rejection of all the religious instruction they ever received, without ever seriously examining it, giving in to the fierce urge to shake it off. (p. 38–9)

I think it is not hard to see how Giussani's characterization of the results of rationalistic education provides a quite accurate analysis of what has happened in America. Those in the "religious right," for example, attempt to protect their religious convictions by supporting "democracy" but thereby fail to see that the form of life they are supporting often has the effect of undermining their faith. This occurs because they are forced to compartmentalize their lives, assuming that "faith" must be protected from the rationalism they rightly think is dominating the wider culture. Their very defence of Christianity too often makes the Christian faith appear to be a counter-rationalistic system. I often think the people in the "religious right" are like canaries in coal mines. They rightly see something is wrong, but they fail to see that their own account of the Christian faith has been shaped by their enemies.

Alasdair MacIntyre's account of compartmentalization nicely complements Giussani's analysis of the results of how rationalism leads to skepticism. MacIntyre observes that

the graduates of the best research universities tend to become narrowly focused professionals, immensely and even obsessively hard-working, disturbingly competitive and intent on success as it is measured within their own specialized professional sphere, often genuinely excellent at what they do; who read little worthwhile that is not relevant to their work; who, as the idiom insightfully puts it, "make time," sometimes with difficulty, for their family lives; and whose relaxation tends to consist of short strenuous bouts of competitive athletic activity and sometimes of therapeutic indulgence in the kind of religion that is well designed not to disrupt their working lives.[20]

Such lives are compartmentalized in at least two ways: (1) it is assumed that an individual passes through various spheres each with its own norms, so the self is but a collection of different roles, which (2) makes it impossible for the individual ever to view her or his life as a whole.[21]

The fragmentation of the curriculum, therefore, becomes the institutional expression of the compart- mentalized character of modern societies necessary to legitimate the form of life thought required to sustain democratic societies. For it is assumed that the kinds of lives produced by modern university curricula will be critical of everything, believing in nothing. Yet, if Giussani is right that skepticism is the breeding ground of fanaticism, then it is by no means clear that the rationalism that is the ideology of modern democratic regimes will be successful.

Modern democratic theory has been an attempt to give an account of democracies as just, without the people that constitute such a society having the virtue of justice. Of course, liberal democratic societies do form people in certain virtues (e.g., cynicism), but they seldom do so explicitly. The kind of training in virtue liberal educational practice involves cannot be acknowledged, because the neutrality that allegedly is required for education to be for anyone makes it impossible to make candid that any education is a moral education. It is unclear, however, if the kind of fragmented selves such an education produces are capable of being habituated in a manner necessary to sustain the virtues to form people of character.

These are obviously large issues, but they are at the heart of Giussani's account of the kind of education required by the Christian faith. I think, moreover, he is right to suggest that the education he is advocating can provide a more defensible account of democracy than that based on the rationalism of modernity. Indeed I find it quite interesting that Giussani, like Pope John Paul II, is not afraid to say that what is required if we are to live in peace with one another is a "civilization of love." (Encyclical letter *Centesimus Annus*, section I, no. 10)

To suggest that nothing less than love is at the heart of our contemporary challenges will no doubt be interpreted by many as an indication that Giussani has lost touch with reality. But that is the case only if you think the God Christians worship is not the God of Jesus Christ. Because as Christians we find our lives constituted by the confidence God gives us that the truth matters, we can continue – as Luigi Giussani argues we must – to take the "risk of education."

Preface

The basic idea behind the education of young people is that society is rebuilt through them. For this
reason, the large-scale issue of society on the whole
is, first of all, a matter of educating the young (the
opposite of how it tends to be approached today).

The chief topic for us, in all our discussions, is
education: how to educate ourselves, what makes an
education, and how is it carried out – an *education*
that is *true*; that is, which corresponds to humanity. It
is education of what is *human*, of the original element
present in all of us. Each of us manifests this element
differently, even if the heart is always essentially and
fundamentally the same. Indeed, in its multitude of
expressions, in the variety of cultures and habits, the
human heart is *one*. My heart is your heart, and it is
the same heart shared by those who live far from us,
in other countries and on other continents.

The primary concern of a true and sufficient education is that of *educating the human heart as God made
it*. Morality is nothing more than making the original

attitude with which God created human beings, with respect to all things and in relationship with them, continue on.

Of all the things one should say about education, these points are of utmost importance.

1. Education requires an *adequate proposal of the past*. Without proposing the past, without an awareness of the past, of tradition, young people grow convoluted or skeptical. If no proposal is made of a privileged working hypothesis, young people will invent one for themselves, in a convoluted way, or else become skeptical. And skepticism is the far easier route, because there they can avoid making even the effort necessary to consistently apply whichever hypothesis they choose.

In *Realtà e giovinezza: La sfida* (Reality and Youth: The Challenge), I wrote: "Knowingly embracing tradition offers a holistic view of reality. It offers a hypothesis concerning meaning and an image of destiny." People come into the world with an image of destiny, with a hypothesized meaning not yet contained in books. It is the heart, as we said before. "[T]radition is like a working hypothesis," the text goes on, "which nature uses to launch people into the comparison against all things."[1]

2. The second need concerns the fact that the past may only be proposed to young people if it is presented *within a present, lived experience* that underscores its correspondence with the ultimate needs of

the heart. That is to say: within a present experience that offers reasons accounting for itself. Only an experience of this kind is capable of proposing, and has the right and duty to propose, tradition, the past. But if the past does not enter the scene, if it is not proposed in the context of a present experience that attempts to provide its reasons for being, then it will also be impossible to attain the third thing that is necessary for education: criticism.

3. True education must be *education to criticism*.

Up until ten years of age (or perhaps younger now), children can still say: "My teacher said so. My mom said so." Why? Because anyone who loves a child will put in their backpack, on their shoulders, all the best things they have experienced and chosen in life. Then, at a certain point, nature gives the child, the former child, the instinct to pull the pack around and place it before their eyes (the Greek word is *probállo*, from which we get the English word *problem*). What others have told us must become a *problem*! If it does not become a problem, it will never mature, and we will either irrationally abandon it or irrationally cling to it.

Once we have brought the pack around before our eyes, we sift through what is inside. In Greek this sifting is called *krinein*, *krísis* – the root of *criticism*. Criticism means taking stock of the reasons for things. It does not necessarily have a negative connotation.

So young people will sift through the pack and, with this criticism, will compare everything they find inside (that is, everything that tradition has placed on their shoulders) against the desires of their heart. Indeed, the ultimate criterion for judgment is inside of us; otherwise we are alienated. And the ultimate criterion, which is each one of us, is identical: it is the need for what is true, beautiful, and good. In spite of, or through, any possible differences that the imagination can draw from these needs, they remain fundamentally identical in their movements, even if the characteristics of the circumstances of the experience differ.

Our insistence is on *critical education*. Kids receive from the past through a present experience that they encounter, and which proposes that past to them, offering reasons in support of it. But they have to take this past and these reasons and lift them before their eyes, compare them with their own heart, and say, "It's true," or "It's not true," or "I doubt it." Thus, with the support of a companionship (without this companionship, people are too much at the mercy of the winds of their hearts, in the negative and instinctive sense of the word), they can say, "Yes," or "No." In doing so, they acquire their features as a person.

We have been too afraid of this criticism, truly we have. And those who are not too afraid have applied it without knowing what it was, and have failed to apply it well. Criticism has been reduced to negativity, so that people take issue with anything that is said to them. Say I tell you something. Now, for you to ask a question about it, to say to yourself, "Is it true?" has become tantamount to doubting what I have said. Equating problem and doubt is the disaster ailing the minds of young people.

Doubt is the end of the investigation (whether temporary or otherwise). The problem, on the other hand, is the invitation to understand what you have in front of you, to discover a new good, a new truth. It is an invitation to draw a fuller and more mature level of satisfaction from it.

Tradition, *present experience* which proposes and provides reasons, and *criticism*: if any one of these elements is missing – I am so grateful to my father for having trained me to ask for the reasons for everything; he would say to me each night at bedtime: "You have got to ask yourself why. Ask yourself why" (he had his own reasons for telling me that!) – young people become frail leaves, far removed from their branch ("Where are you going?" Leopardi asked).[2] They become victims of the prevailing winds and their changeability – victims of a general public opinion created by the current power.

We want to free young people (this is our purpose). We want to free them from mental slavery, from the homogenization that mentally turns others into slaves.

Since my first hour in the classroom I have always said: "I am not here to make you adopt the ideas I will give you as your own, but to teach you a true method for judging the things I will say. And the things that I will say are an experience, which is the outcome of a long past: two thousand years."

Respect for this method has defined our commitment to education since the beginning, clearly indicating its purpose: to demonstrate how faith is relevant to life's needs. Because of my formation at home and in seminary, first, and my own reflections later, I was deeply convinced that, unless faith could be found and located in present experience, and confirmed by it, and useful for responding to its needs, it would not be able to endure in a world where everything, *everything*, said and says the opposite. So much so that even theology has been a victim of this collapse for a long time now.

Demonstrating the relevance of faith for the needs of life and, therefore (this "therefore" is important for me), demonstrating the reasonableness of faith, implies a precise idea of reason. To say that faith exalts reason means that faith corresponds to the fundamental and original needs of the heart of each person. Indeed, the Bible uses the word *heart* instead of the word *reason*. Thus, faith responds to the original needs of the human heart, which are the same in everyone: the needs for truth, goodness, justice (what is just!), love, and total self-satisfaction, which (as I often emphasize to the kids) means the same thing indicated by the word *perfection* (*satisfacere* or *satisfieri* in Latin is similar to the word *perficere*, perfection; perfection and satisfaction are the same thing, just as happiness and eternity are the same thing).

So, when we say reason, we mean the fact of corresponding to the fundamental needs of the human heart. Every person, willing or unwilling, and whether they know it or not, judges everything with these fundamental needs. They ultimately judge everything, perfectly or imperfectly.

For this reason, unpacking the reasons for faith means describing ever more thoroughly, ever more fully, ever more densely, the effects of the presence of Christ in the life of the Church in its authenticity, the Church whose "sentinel" is the pope in Rome. What faith proposes, therefore, is transformation of life.

Where we go wrong is when we understand, propose, and live faith as a premise that is not maintained, a premise that has nothing to do with life. With life: life is today, because yesterday is gone and tomorrow is not here yet. Life is today. I go so far as to tell the kids that anything that has absolutely nothing to do with my experience today, with my present experience, does not exist. It simply does not exist. So a God who has nothing to do with what I am experiencing, here and now, has no place at all. There is no such God. That's a God who does not exist, a Christ who does not exist, a Body of Christ that does not exist. Maybe it's there in the head of some theologian, but it is not in me – it cannot be in me.

The separation of heaven from the earth is the crime that rendered the religious sense, or, more correctly, the religious sentiment, vague and abstract, like a cloud skimming along in the sky that quickly dissipates, wears thin, and vanishes. Meanwhile the earth remains ultimately dominated by pride (willingly or unwillingly), just as it was with Adam and Eve, by self-imposition, and by violence. Elio Toaff, the chief rabbi of Rome, wrote in a recent book: "The messianic age is precisely the opposite of the one called for by Christianity. We [Jews] want to bring God back down to earth, not bring man to the heavens. We do not give the kingdom of heaven to human beings; we want God to return to reign on earth."[3] When I read this sentence I leapt up onto my chair! This precisely describes the character of the charism with which we see and feel Christianity, because Christianity is "God on earth." And the whole purpose of our work and our lives is the glory of Christ, the glory of the man Christ, of the man–God Christ. The glory of Christ is a temporal thing, which belongs to time and space and to history. It is within history, on this side of the ultimate limit, because on the other side He alone takes care of giving him glory. On the other side, his glory overlaps with eternity, but here, if I do not serve him, His glory is less.

When I was in high school and would listen to what my spiritual fathers had to say (especially Fr. Motta, a keen little old man), what impressed me most of all was this sentence: "If you do not make sacrifices, do not pray as you should, and do not do your duty, the glory of Christ is less." The idea that I could diminish Christ's glory humiliated me. This means that they had already succeeded in communicating to me the experience of old men – the experience of mature men, that is, great in faith. They had already communicated to me love for Christ.

In Dvořák's *Stabat Mater* (which is nearly as lovely as Pergolesi's), the basses sing, "*Fac ut ardeat cor meum in amando Christum Deum ut sibi complaceam*" (Allow my heart to be kindled with love for Christ God, so it will be pleasing to him). Since one of the features of this

Stabat Mater is the indistinct repetition of phrases, I was struck by this verse, because I saw in it the thing that painfully separates me from the vast majority of the people around me. *Ut ardeat* ... the totality of Christ's imposing presence, so totalizing that it becomes the law of our daily actions. "In the experience of a great love," Romano Guardini wrote, "everything becomes an event within its scope."[4] Everything. If it rains or if it's a beautiful day; if a thing goes well or goes all wrong; work, peace, music, breathing, illness ... Everything becomes an event within its scope. This is true of our love for a man or a woman when it is strong, and sincere, and transparent. It is true of the love we have for a friend – it's the same. If faith indicates the involvement of God with the human now (now, the human now!), then we can readily understand a statement like Guardini's.

Chapter two of St. Paul's letter to the Galatians says: "[I]nsofar as I now live in the flesh [Flesh is what is defined in time and space. It defines itself in the contingent], I live by faith in the Son of God who has loved me and given himself up for me."[5] Can we conceive of any faith without this emotion that comes from a present experience (tomorrow it will be a present experience happening tomorrow!)? We originated from the following persuasion: faith cannot be understood differently. Otherwise it would be absurd, and belonging to it would be absurd! Every friend who follows me senses this. You can make mistakes and be inconsistent a thousand times. You can be a sinner like me. But the path is this one.

I remember the first class I taught in high school: it was the E section for first-year students at Berchet. I was about to go up to the podium when I saw a hand go up in the back of the room, on the left (way in the back, the very last desk). And I thought, "Oh boy, problems already, and we haven't even started yet!" [Out loud I said:] "Yes, go ahead" (and I saw on the class roll that the boy's name was Pavesi – I remember it perfectly well forty years later!). "Professor, it's pointless to come in here and talk about religion[," he said, "]Because in order to talk one needs to use reason – you need to use reason. And using reason when it comes to faith is pointless because they are skew lines: the two never intersect. Reason can say one thing, and faith another. They're two different worlds!"

I was caught somewhat off guard by this question, which I frankly hadn't expected, but I said, "Pardon me, but what is faith?" He looked around – his classmates chortled. So I turned and put it directly to the entire class: "Who here knows what faith is? Who can describe it, define it, tell it to me, or put it any way you want?" The whole group became serious, and no one answered.

I worked up the nerve and said [to him], in a stronger voice, "Tell me, please, what is reason?" Same reaction. So I turned again to the class: "What is reason?!" No one gave an answer.

So at that point (naturally) I kicked it into high gear and said to the group, "Seriously? You talk about faith and reason without even knowing the meaning of those words? It's an embarrassment. You're better than that! You're young, you're supposed to enter into life with clarity, with sincerity. When you don't know something you should say, 'I don't know,' not make pronouncements, not make judgments!" I went to leave the classroom and bumped into the philosophy teacher, Professor Miccinesi, whom, during the debate, I had thought might have been the root of this situation with the students. I told him: "Professor, these kids are a bit disloyal, without meaning to be, because they use words without knowing their meaning, and use them to make judgments." He asked what I was talking about, so I told him. He replied, "They're right." "What? You, too?" I asked. And he said, "The second Arausican Council said that faith and reason are contrary to one another." "Look," I replied, "I spent a few years teaching theology, and that is one thing that I certainly don't remember ever having to communicate to the seminarians. And if I ever did communicate it, I would now say that I was crazy. But you are a historian – surely you know that the historical method demands that the meaning of the words in a little piece of an argument, in a few paragraphs lifted off a page, must be assessed within the context of the climate of knowledge and the mentality that prevailed in a particular time period." I used this analogy for the kids: if I were to say *Il faut se coucher avec les poules*, someone who did not speak French would be shocked by this advice to go sleep with chickens … or at least think it was bizarre. But a French speaker would know that it's just an expression. [At this point] I had to leave, and the entire class was crammed into the hallway (if the principal had come by, he would have taken us to task!), so I said to the other teacher (because I didn't want to leave without giving the kids something to understand, at least one thought to take away), "Listen, Professor, I swear that you are in front of me – is this rational or not?" He replied, "Yes, it's clear to you." "And," I went on, "I swear and, with equal certainty, state that America exists, although I've never seen it" (at the time I thought I never would see it, but unfortunately I ended up going there many times – too many times!). "At this moment I say that America exists, regardless of whether tomorrow, or someday, I am ever able to go there. Do you think this is reasonable or not?" He chose (like Ugo Spirito in a famous debate with Bontadini at the San Fedele centre)[6] to be consistent with himself, and he answered, "No, it would not be reasonable." "There you have it, kids," I exclaimed. "The difference between myself and your philosophy teacher is not that I believe and he doesn't, or that I believe and you don't. It's that I have an idea of reason that says that the existence of America is rationally preferable, reasonably affirmable, right now, by me. For him, it's not. So watch out, all of you, be careful with your teacher," (I was still saying everything right in front of him) "be wary of him, because he can lead you to have an idea of reason where stating that America exists without ever having seen it is unreasonable, while stating that the person right before your eyes exists is reasonable. I am even more sure that America exists than I am that he is standing before my eyes." This was how I introduced the idea of "moral certainty."

With this example I mean to underscore that, if faith had nothing to do with reason, faith could have nothing to do with life, because reason is the distinctive way in which human beings live.

The points I have laid out have been the heart of the entire theoretical framework of the Movement that God has given me the grace of seeing. This Movement originated from a taste for reason, a taste for understanding reason clearly, and a taste for reliving it constantly in the present moment. And the Movement has been fairly alone in this, in the cultural context then as now, because the culture today is based on weak reason and nihilism, while we asserted the power and revealing corporality of the sign. Weak reason and nihilism are not the only realities; there is also the mysterious, but real, phenomenon of a reality that is the sign of another, which is capable of being experienced. Faith is the exaltation of the sign, of the value of the sign. Thus the reason between us became the search for an authentic way to grasp reality by judging what happened, grasping the correspondence to the needs that made up our souls, or our hearts, as the Bible puts it. We made this translation of the old scholastic adage: the truth is an *adaequatio rei et intellectus*,[7] a correspondence between the object and our self-awareness; our awareness of ourselves – that is, the awareness of the needs that make up our hearts, that make up the person, without which the person would be nothing!

Thus faith is proposed as the supreme rationality. Put this way, the phrase may be open to criticism, but it is important to understand what is meant by it. Faith is placed at the top of the supreme apex of rationality: when it reaches its apex in the study of a thing, in the sentiment of a thing, our human nature senses that there is something more. This defines the concept of sign: our nature senses that what it experiences, what it has at hand, refers to something else. We have called this the "vanishing point." It is the vanishing point that exists in every human experience; that is, a point that does not close, but rather refers beyond. This is another crucial concept in all our teaching.

Thus, faith is proposed as the supreme rationality to the extent that the encounter with the event that carries it generates an experience and a correspondence to our humanity that is otherwise unthinkable.

When John and Andrew went to Jesus' house that afternoon, and stayed there to watch him speak, they went back home saying: "We have found the Messiah." And the text does not say what he said. Who knows what they understood from what he said! But it was clear to them that there was no one else like that man, because he was something beyond. And this is the question they asked him some time later, when He made the miracle that immediately calmed the stormy sea. And his disciples (who knew who his mother and father were, knew his brothers, knew where he lived; they knew everything about Him because they had been close for months already) were frightened, and asked each other: "Who is this man?" There was such a gross mismatch between what that man was and what they could think, imagine, and expect, that they could find no explanation: it was beyond reason. This is the process through which faith happens in me, in you, and in whomever else, with the grace of God, of course! And this is the thing that was missing for my great "friend" from my youth: Leopardi, the poet who, with me, is known to all my friends.

I remember the third year of gymnasium (eighth grade), when I first had an intuition of all these things. It was not my professors who explained them to me. I understood them from reading Leopardi's poem "To His Lady," in which he addresses beauty with an inspired hymn. Not the beauty of this one woman, or that one (or any of the lovers he had), but beauty with a capital B, of which he says:

No hope of seeing you alive
remains for me now,
except when, naked and alone,
my soul will go down a new street
to an unfamiliar home.
Already, at the dawning
of my dark, uncertain day
I imagined you a fellow traveller
on this parched ground. But no thing on earth
compares with you; and if someone
who had a face like yours resembled you
in word and deed, still she would be less lovely.

"Except when … ," when you entered another world, another earth … Reading this poem in the third year of gymnasium (in May of the third year of gymnasium), I understood that Leopardi had had the intuition. And, indeed, the ode "To His Lady" ends with that soaring line "Whether you are the one and only eternal idea [if you are one of the ideas of Plato, o Beauty, and live on some star], […] / or if in the supernal spheres another earth / from among unnumbered worlds receives you, / [in other worlds] […] From here, where years are both ill-starred and brief / accept this hymn from your unnoticed lover."[8] What?! "Unnoticed lover," to her, to one present among us: beauty made human, flesh – *flesh!* – and unknown to us all. She did not refuse to carry this mortal flesh, but did carry mortal flesh among us; she carries it among us, and we are far from her. In short, I said, "This is chapter one of St. John: 'The Word became flesh.'"[9]

This was the most decisive moment in my cultural existence. I say "cultural," since faith is related to reason. And, already at that time, I intuited roughly the same thing that I said above: that faith responds to the needs of the heart more than any other hypothesis. That is why it is more reasonable than any other rational hypothesis.

Faith is proposed as the supreme rationality to the extent that the encounter with the event that carries it generates an experience and a correspondence to our humanity that is unthought-of, unthinkable.

This intuition from the third year of gymnasium was confirmed for me when I read Giulio Augusto

Levi's essay on Leopardi in preparation for the maturity exam.[10] Imagine my surprise when I reached the part where Levi says that the ode "To His Lady" was the peak of Leopardi's trajectory, after which he slid toward "La ginestra." He was not able to endure, and he had no one around him, no friendships, no companionship that would have pushed and supported him in making the tiny step he would have had to make: the step to make the comparison with the first chapter of St. John. What you hoped for in that hymn to beauty, which, when you were little, you hoped to find on the streets of this road, really did occur: it is the Christian announcement. It is the Christian message. And the most famous commentator at the time supported this interpretation.

Some time ago, a friend went to interview the last descendent of Leopardi. She told him that she didn't want to see another critic or journalist, because no one understood Leopardi. For this reason alone she wouldn't talk to him – and she had a point! As she was saying the last word, he interjected, "Wait – I've read Giulio Augusto Levi." She stopped, turned on her heel, and said, "What? Someone as young as you has read Giulio Augusto Levi? This is the first time anyone has mentioned him to me – he is the only one who interpreted him correctly on that point!"

I tell this story only to point out that this claim of ours is not naïveté. So much so that, the more we speak, and the more time passes, the more passion we have … And the more our hearts are pained by the misery of people, of those who do not know, and we thank God first of all for our mothers, because without them the Church would not have reached us.

"Among them they have a respect that others cannot understand," the *Letter to Diognetus* says.[11] *Respect.* Based on its root, this word means looking at something "sideways," taking stock of something else from the corner your eye. It means looking at everything there is perceiving the presence of an other, looking at the presence of an other. In short, a person's life may be riddled with errors, mistakes, and inconsistencies, but their life as a Christian is faith, and faith is this: awareness of a presence within the orbit of any present experience.

"There is a goal," Kafka said, "but no way."[12] This is another important passage. Faith is the way to what reason searches for more than any other thing. Ultimately, what is reason looking for if not the meaning of life, the meaning of existence, the meaning of everything? And all of contemporary philosophy is resigned to saying: could there be a meaning? The three hundred people who walked with our great Cardinal Martini represented three hundred different religions,[13] but all of them expressed the presence of a meaning – just like the line from Kafka. The meaning exists but is so mysterious that we don't know how to think of it – there is no way!

Two thousand years ago, the meaning itself came among us to say: "I am the way and the truth and the life."[14] He was the only man to say such a thing in the history of the world!

Permit me to add just one final point. Faith is about an event that must be experienced, not read or talked about. An event must be lived out, otherwise our way of facing it is insufficient. The great exegete Heinrich Schlier said, in one of his well-known books: "The ultimate and particular meaning of an event, and, thus, the event itself in its authenticity, opens itself [that is, communicates itself] only and always to an experience that may abandon itself to it and, in this abandonment, may attempt to interpret it."[15] "To an experience": an event appears to those who participate in experiencing it. It appears only to an experience that is authentic, if the experience is adequate to the event in question. The event at issue is that God became flesh, became man, and is present: "I am with you always, until the end of the age."[16] He is present! He is present every day! We need to abandon ourselves to this message and approach experience in accordance with the traits of the message. He says that he will be present every day in the community of believers, who he gathers and makes into His mysterious Body. We must abandon ourselves to this presence and live our life within this presence, live it under the influence of this presence, judged by this presence, enlightened by this presence, and sustained by this presence.

Christianity is an event: we submit our entire life to it, our entire life in the instant. Just as, as Guardini said, "in the experience of a great love, everything becomes an event within its scope," so must we subject our entire life story to the Christian event.

I would like to emphasize one last thing. By nature, an approach like this one is ecumenical.

A concept of faith in its relationship to reason like the one here described (faith is the final answer to what human beings experience as the supreme need for which they are made, to which reason cannot and does not know how to find an answer; nevertheless, if followed, reason leads us to the point of saying: "This refers beyond to something else. Thus it is a sign. Everything is a sign of something else!") together with, in the second place, the idea of Christianity as an event (for which the great law for understanding faith, since it is "the cause" of an event, of an occurrence, not a word or a thought, is participating in the event itself, as sufficiently as we can, and asking God to make us capable of participating), both these things foster what now seems to be the most ponderous and serious word of the entire topic of religion: *ecumenism*. By nature, Christianity is ecumenical and Christian faith is ecumenical. Claiming to be the truth, not only is it not unafraid of new comparisons, but, above all, it extracts what is true from every encounter, gleaning what already belonged to it, constructing its own face in history with a magnanimity that looks at the true aspect in everything it meets, and exalts it, and says if it is just, if it is good, if it is true. And it builds itself with everything it meets, excluding nothing, judging nothing. It affirms what was given to it. It affirms that which it is.

Conversely, if one is aware that what they have is not the truth, but an image of truth that is arguable or debatable, they cannot help but defend themselves. They put themselves on the defensive and abandon the rest (in the best of cases) to tolerance. But we are accustomed to look at everything, *every thing*, for that bit of goodness that it may have inside and to exalt it, to feel a sense of affinity for it, and to perceive it as a travelling companion. Thus, it is a universal embrace. This is what makes people start to come together. Being together, what young people begin when they have a family, is an embrace that expands. It does not shrink inward, but expand outward to all the world, and, by its nature, suffers for the world, hurts for the world, and participates in Christ's suffering on the cross for the world. And it perceives the resurrection, the pulse of the resurrection, in whatever is good, anywhere and in anyone.

Veritas Domini manet in aeternum:[17] what is true endures forever. This is our idea of ecumenism, and, in this, we feel that we are thoroughly disciples of Cardinal Martini, because he recalls us to this magnanimity in everything he says. But also because "ecumenism" is our true concept of culture. The first Christians did not use the word *culture*; they started out using this other word, *oikouméne*, "ecumenism." Culture is a principle from which we try to understand all the rest, to the extent we can, building in whatever way we can. The principle that makes us embrace everything, the origin of this magnanimity is Christ present among us, Christ experienced among us: faith.

Thus we understand how the Christian faith entered into the world at that time, where the Pax

Romana reigned, but where there was an enormous distance between people, and the law of relationships was violence (whether a little or a lot, it was violence). Christianity came in bringing *eirene*, peace. Because Christ is our peace, and this is what we hope for most, as both a promise and a foretaste: the promise of eternity, and peace in the place where we live together.

The Risk of Education

Introductory Thoughts

I. A Matter of Method

Italy in the late-1950s: The birth of an intuition

At first glance, Italy in the 1950s seemed to offer the ideal environment for the transmission of Catholic teaching on theory and ethics. The parishes were well run and offered catechism courses "for all seasons." Religion classes were mandatory in all elementary and middle schools. Families served to preserve tradition, at least in theory, in the values they handed down. There was still a degree of reluctance to accept sweeping criticism of religion and irreligious information. Sunday Mass attendance was high, and so on. But even preliminary contact with Italian high school students of that day would have immediately introduced the interested observer to three revealing facts.

First of all, faith was not ultimately grounded in any rational basis. St. Augustine provides us with an apt image in his *Sermons*, where he uses reading as a symbol to evoke the positive certainty of faith grounded in reason:

As he who sees letters in an excellently written manuscript, and knows not how to read, praises indeed the transcriber's hand, and admires the beauty of the characters; but what those characters mean or signify he does not know; and by the sight of his eyes he is a praiser of the work, but in his mind has no comprehension of it; whereas another man both praises the work, and is capable of understanding it; such a one, I mean, who is not only able to see what is common to all, but who can read also; which he who has never learned cannot.[1]

Second, it was taken for granted that faith had nothing to do with social behaviour in general, and behaviour at school in particular.

Finally, there was an environment that undeniably generated skepticism, and which opened the door for certain teachers to attack religion. Those who did so easily earned a certain respectful regard from the students and fostered a profound apathy in them, the first practical repercussion of which was a loss of ethics.

It was a situation that seemed to present an inevitable either-or choice: either one had to conclude that Christianity had lost all its persuasive power and relevance for the lives of young students, or else one had to conclude that the Christian fact was not being presented or offered to them in an adequate way.

Accepting the first hypothesis would have been a clear endorsement of the historical judgment made by Gramsci, but it was evident that the clarity and energy of a lived Christian faith could not give in to what that cultural view suggested.

Therefore, we could conclude that the issue of communicating (and developing) the traditional content could be considered, above all, a problem of method.

This insight rested upon two pillars.

The first was theoretical in nature: the fact that the contents of faith must be embraced through reason. That is, they should be presented in their capacity to improve, illuminate, and enhance authentic human values.

The second pillar can be expressed by saying that this presentation must be verified in action. That is, rational evidence can reach the point of conviction only in the experience of a human need addressed from within participation in the Christian fact; and this participation means involvement with the Christian reality as a fundamentally social or communional act.

The test of risk

This method runs an obvious risk in its insistence on the rationality of the project of faith: it cannot claim to be a mathematical or apodictic proof.

And there is a risk in saying that conviction may only arise from experience. This is not a matter of evoking certain feelings or stirring up some pietistic emotion. Rather, it is a genuine engagement that cannot cheat us. Thus, experience places us at the mercy of the quicksand of our freedom. A relevant quote from Hans Urs von Balthasar comes to mind: "He understands that, in order to understand, he must recreate the truth in himself in a living manner. This is how he becomes a 'disciple.' He commits himself and entrusts himself to the 'way.'"[2]

On the other hand, if they do not take the test of risk, educator and pupil alike will be starting from a fiction: a supposed mystery that is actually reducible to visual evidence, and an imagined freedom, which is really a mechanical reaction to every stimulus that comes along.

A journey that is shared by educator and pupil

The first step

The first way to move is to be moved; that is, to move oneself together with the Presence that revealed itself, the Word of God.

God is our "definitiveness" in the fullest sense of that word. Not just in the finalistic sense, but as our very definition. In Genesis we read: "Let us make human beings in our image, after our likeness."[3]

Now, this is precisely what human beings do not accept. The entire question of religion is wrapped up in this statement. The question of the truth and falsehood of life can be found here, and here alone.

We often tend to reduce our idea of ourselves to whether we have complied with certain rules, and we define ourselves on that basis. But according to Christian tradition, this is precisely what sin is: the fact of identifying our own definitiveness with an idol; that is, with a form, with something domitable, something that can be understood in its entirety, a construct designed to provide us with a sense of security. This is why moralism is idolatry. In reality, it is an imposter of moral life reduced to looking for certainties in what one does or does not do.

Saying that a human being's definitiveness is God means, on the contrary, that the definition of human beings and their destiny is *mystery*. This means fixing, as the ordinary horizons of existence, this powerful suggestion from the Bible:

> Let the wicked forsake their way,
> and sinners their thoughts;
> Let them turn to the Lord to find mercy;
> to our God, who is generous in forgiving.
> For my thoughts are not your thoughts,
> nor are your ways my ways – oracle of the Lord.
> For as the heavens are higher than the earth,
> so are my ways higher than your ways,
> my thoughts higher than your thoughts.[4]

But we human beings tend to run away both from contemplating the fact that our definitiveness is the mystery of God and from evidence of our sins. We need help to take on this contemplation and this evidence; we need support to avoid running away.

The word *mystery* indicates something incommensurable with us. This is not to say that it is "different," since we who are made in His image carry a reverberation or echo of many aspects within ourselves. But even when it comes to these aspects, the modality, the ultimate way, the decisive measure with which they come into being and their final criterion are not ours. Adhering to them always requires that we step outside of ourselves, that we pass beyond the dialect in which we are brought to perceive a thing. Even when we try to adhere to them according to an image that our intention seeks to render as purely and obediently as possible, this adherence always and only comes about through a detachment from the self. This is because we cannot claim to be just on the basis of what we do. Our actions still need His mercy in order for us to have hope and certainty of salvation.

Morality is a tension – a tending toward. If it were the "accomplishment" of something, it would no longer be tension. Of course we try to do what we ought to do! But to say that morality is a tension means taking a position always geared toward something else, and open to being corrected in order to penetrate more deeply into a reality that is greater than we are, "as the heavens are higher than the earth." We cannot be pleased with anything we do, as Jesus said in the Gospel: "When you have done all you have been commanded, say, 'We are unprofitable servants.'"[5] The only thing we can be pleased about is affirming Him, or *tending* toward him. Thus, we are totally poor, because humans are nothing before the mystery of God, and their substance is to enter into this relationship, to obey Him instant by instant. It is not possible for us to define what God will ask of us in the next instant of our lives. Just as the quote from Isaiah reminded us, His ways are not our ways and His thoughts are not our thoughts.

Our security lies only in the mystery

All of human religiosity, then, is engaged in recognizing that the one, total meaning of life is the mystery of God. Thus, the meaning of our life exceeds us, is enigmatic to us. The religiosity of human beings is entirely wrapped up in the fact that our security (goodness itself, the good that "makes it all worthwhile") is the mystery. And there is no other thing in which all of human religiosity can play out, not even in following moral rules, because goodness is the mystery we participate in when we respond to the Christian vocation. We must look beyond the level of the tools or structures that embody our response and refuse to base our certainty and trust on them. Security is, exclusively, the fact of following Him, because He is the substance of our life.

We tend to identify even Christ with a mental, imaginative, and, in the final analysis, sentimental form, while really Christ is a Man who is mystery; a mystery that does not keep its distance, that is not confined to the heavens, but that appears before our daily life in its intimate details: when we eat, when we drink, when we rest, when we run into unexpected difficulties. It is the mystery that enters into our relationships with people, into our homes; the mystery that meets us face-to-face at exactly the moment when we would like to do one thing but must do another instead; and that questions and provokes us in the most pressing matters, in what we hold most dear. And in this provocation we are reminded once again that, "My ways are not your ways."

It is the mystery that, despite the fact that we are constantly living out the idolatry of our certainties, offers itself to us constantly to the point of death. St. John's Gospel tells us: "He loved his own in the world and he loved them to the end."[6]

The journey that educator and pupil are called to take together is the journey of explicitly running the risk of accepting the call and the challenge of this definition of ourselves, of the mystery that invites us to recognize ourselves as made by Him. And it is in this common journey, defined by the definitive end-point of destiny, that we come to know the features of our path.

From a method, a movement

"He loved them to the end," we said.

The fact that He died means that He is there in any situation that affects us, and in anything we do; He does not draw back. He is the mercy and compassion that will prevail upon us in the end. Thus, our opportunity to be true is in this limitless mercy and compassion. If there is a possibility for a human being to change, this possibility is the presence of limitless mercy and compassion in this world.

It is impossible for our minds to truly comprehend what it means to say, "My salvation is Christ," just as it is impossible to "naturally" understand that the definition of ourselves is another. More precisely, it is inconceivable to us that our own transformations and our own becoming true occur by another's compassion and mercy.

It is neither obvious nor likely that, in a society like ours, people will be helped to comprehend these things, because they are not rational points in the naturalistic sense of that word. They are the sum total of reason; that is to say, the mind of the creature taking part in the mind of God.

To be brief, one might say that the method of a movement is what emerges from the points and insights laid out at the beginning. It consists in seeking and helping to build the life conditions that facilitate the progress of this understanding.

II. The Personal Dimension and the Community Dimension

A value must inevitably become embodied

Just as it is true that human beings cannot base their security on any of the forms that embody the mystery for them, it is also true that any good that does not at least attempt to take on an embodied form will inevitably disappear over time.

For this reason, the embodied form has all the importance of the good itself, because it embraces its full dignity. For Christians, not one millimetre of mismatch should be measured between the form in its most minute and trivial details (like the humblest and seemingly least important of jobs) and love for Christ. Our destiny plays out in the place and the instant in which we are living, here and now.

In order to avoid reducing our relationship with our destiny to an abstract statement or a sentimental suggestion, it must be a relationship with a place that becomes a track to destiny itself, to Christ.

In the broad sense, this track is God's Church, but let us ask ourselves: what is God's Church made of? Of people who have been convoked; that is, called together. St. Thomas said, "*Ecclesia est quaedam congregatio*"[7]; that is, "The Church is a congregation." It is an assembly, as the literal meaning of the word *ecclesia* indicates – an assembly that constitutes our being because of the presence of the mystery of Christ, and which educates our being to identify more and more with that mystery. The track of the Church is made up of people who have been called in the same way.

But people exist in a given space, just as they live at a set time, and space and time together are called a place, a context. The relationship with Christ passes through people who build relationships, people who need rooms, chairs, windows, pots and pans and food to cook in them, beds to sleep in – in short, people who need everything required to live. This is why participating in God's Church cannot be reduced to going to Mass when one feels like it (and, therefore, cannot be reduced to something abstract)!

A place to build

We must keep in mind that the place we have been describing – made up of people and things – must be built. We have to build a house before we can move into it. We have to cook a dish before we can taste it. The walls of this place, which make it possible to participate in the mystery and the Church of God, are made up of something called fraternity, reciprocal affection. But how can we live as brothers and sisters with people whom we did not ultimately choose ourselves?

A personal matter

This is an absolutely personal matter. If we consider our nature to be the image of the mystery that made us, to be participation in this mystery, and if we understand that this mystery is mercy and compassion, then we will try to practice mercy, compassion, and fraternity as our very nature, whatever the effort involved.

Without this personal dimension, then, we cannot belong to a place of convocation.

Affirming oneself by recognizing the value of others

This mercy, which takes us as its object and constitutes us, must become a self, a subject. Here I mean the mercy and affection that the mystery of God has for each person. We are so thoroughly the object of this affection that we are made, created, saved, and kept alive by it. Since we are made of this affection, it must become our very self, our subject. All our actions must come from this mercy, or else they betray our deepest nature.

When we act in mercy we recognize the value of others. If we see only one bright spot amid a thousand negatives, we affirm that bright spot. Not because it is a bright spot, but because it is the peephole of the mystery that the other carries inside. This is love: when one's own fulfillment, one's self-realization, coincides with affirming others.

A personal task carried out "suspended" from God

The work of bringing this personal dimension to maturity within ourselves builds the walls of the place that hosts the mystery for us, and through which the mystery reaches us.

This work is personal, and may only be carried out in a position that I would describe as "suspended" from God.

The Bible tells us of an extraordinary episode that exemplifies how we can understand ourselves to be "suspended" from God, from an Other. It is the story in Exodus of the manna that the Lord sends to His people in the desert. He commands the people not to try to stockpile it because, if they do, the providential food will become inedible.

If we truly recognize that the mystery that created all things became one of us, and remained present in history in a way so paradoxical to our mindset, we must also be prepared to recognize, again and again, that His forms are not our forms. Then we will discover that our forms are saved only within His. Otherwise they deteriorate, like the manna in the desert when it was not used in obedience but rather preserved according to the criteria of the people. The Israelites who stored the manna for future days did not truly live the place that was their people, because they forgot that what defined Israel was its recognition of the fact that its very life hung from, was "suspended" from, the mystery that is the truth in the world. Like them, we, too, will fail to create or belong to any entity that wishes to testify to the mystery unless we have a personal education that assimilates us more and more to the merciful mystery that made us and saved us, and unless we have a personal dimension whose trust lies only in that mystery.

A community matter

In addition to the personal dimension, this is also a community matter, a communitarian issue, as the points laid out above make clear. For Christians, the value of their person consists in the Body of Christ that grows, in the mystery of Christ present in His Church. Thus, we establish ourselves by establishing the Church.

Other people are to be "hosted" within ourselves. Hospitality is making another person a part of our own living. Bear in mind that hospitality is the greatest possible sacrifice after that of giving one's life. For this reason, we rarely know how to truly welcome and host others, and do not even know how to welcome ourselves. To make others a part of our own life is the true imitation of Christ, who welcomed us so thoroughly into His life that he made us into parts of His Body. The mystery of Christ's body is the mystery of our body being hosted within His.

The origin of a different speck of humanity

Within the possibility of hosting inside ourselves the other people given to us by Christ (because it is Christ who unites us, as the Gregorian antiphon says: *Congregavit nos in unum Christi amor*,[8] "the love of Christ has called us together into a single thing"), it is possible for a "piece" of a different humanity to become visible, a humanity in which human beings may begin to breathe fully. These beginnings of a new earth are part of the Body of Christ, and all our passion (whatever we may do, be it hammering a nail into the wall or shouldering the greatest responsibilities), all of it serves the purpose of expanding this piece of earth.

We cannot overlook the fact that an educational path must involve these two issues and dimensions: personal and communitarian. Nor can we ignore the effort and self-sacrifice that are demanded by our positive tension toward involving both dimensions.

Moreover, self-sacrifice to Christ is the content of the most expressive gesture we can make as Christians: the Mass. The Eucharist is an act of Christ's, but it is also an act of "mine." "My" act identifies with Christ's act, while His, in turn, identifies with "mine." *Mine*: the offertory is a gesture of *mine*, the consecration is a gesture of *mine*, and communion consumes and completes this, *my* gesture. Self-sacrifice coincides with the offering of self that is implicit in our recognition that Christ is our whole self, and in our acceptance of Him and attempts to act according to this awareness. It is a different awareness, created and educated by that piece of new world we mentioned before.

"To walk humbly with your God"

Unless we feel that our vocational companionship is a small piece of a new humanity that begins to reveal and become the sign of the mystery that Christ is the substance of everything, and if we do not feel this way about everything we come into contact with every day, how can we live "suspended" from the mystery and, thus, give it glory and bear witness to it? How could we become those supreme artists who make the face of Christ vibrate in the world, and who turn whatever they touch, in the way in which they touch it, into a sign of His mysterious Presence?

Let us recall the words of the prophet Micah:

You have been told, O mortal, what is good,
and what the Lord requires of you:
Only to do justice and to love goodness,
and to walk humbly with your God.[9]

This is transformation, the highest art, which is holiness! Holiness is embracing people and things in a way that transforms this embrace into a journey and a cry — a cry that proclaims that the substance of everything is Christ, just as the embrace itself is not ours but His.

III. Times and Contexts in Implementing a Method

Yesterday and today: Educating people for the risk of using freedom

The culture in Italy in the late '50s and '60s (and perhaps elsewhere in Europe as well) partly helped and partly hindered the existential capacity of young people to take the risk of making their freedom real.

It seems to me that that environment encouraged the use of reason, in the form of taking a critical position. But it was marked by an utter absence of the kind of dense community that could support such a need for criticism and provide it with a proving ground. The proliferation of associations and groups so typical of that time did not offer a companionship that was self-aware of the fact that it could be extremely useful for the dynamic of learning. Community based on associations served only to gather together and preserve certain specific sets of interests.

My impression of today's situation is precisely the opposite. Although young people are, generally speaking, quicker to appeal to reason, passion for rational inquiry and intellectual curiosity are either unsustainable or absent entirely. And while growing value is attributed to companionship as important even for learning, there is, as yet, no clear understanding that the community element is inherent to the subject's very act of knowing.

Constancy of the point of reference

The first chapter ("The Dynamic and Elements of the Educational Event") emphasizes the importance of the function of the educator, which it describes as the "function of consistency." Other expressions may be added alongside this one, which evoke, in connection with the function of the educator, "consistency (or coherence)" and a "permanent criterion for judging all of reality" as the "solid protection of the link [...] between the shifting attitude of the young person and [...] ultimate meaning."[10]

It continues to be obvious today that only when an educator calls students' attention to the same reference point with constancy is it possible to create a stable, and, therefore, fruitful, form of education. But I think we need to add the further observation that reaching this result is not, first of all, a matter of the educator always acting in an ethically consistent way on the practical level. Rather it is one of logical consistency. More precisely, it is a matter of students being able to see the consistency of an ideal in the person of the educator. This consistency is able to demonstrate, more than anything else, that the educator's lessons on matters of principle are capable of becoming reference points for the unfolding of an entire life. If teachers state a theoretical principle but neglect to make it a parameter for the specific judgments they must make in life, then, even if they act in a morally consistent way, students will not see this as proof that it is actually possible to apply the principle. Therefore, they will not take it as a verification of its real validity. What strikes the minds of young people is explicit logicalness. This fixes the terms of the ideal within the fabric of their reason.

Educability: Constancy of youth

In a recent conversation, someone asked me: "How can we stay young?" The answer to this question has parallels with a kind of life I describe later on (in reference to the time of maturity, when teacher and student have the same experience of the world and work "together, side by side, toward a destiny that unites us all") in the following way: "a life, which, as it passes, advances in youth, in 'educability,' and in 'wonder' and being moved by things."[11] As I try to lay out the formula for constant youth, these same elements spring to mind.

Youth is characterized by a sense of purpose. This purpose may be undefined, but the young person senses it, at least, in the form of a fortunate future for what they are currently experiencing. This feeling prevents them from having the stiffness that inhibits plasticity, flexibility, and a degree of freshness in their modes of expression. More precisely, the residual sense of mystery, which defines life's horizons and perspective without delimiting them, and generates openness (of one's own limbs, so to speak) to adapt to new scenarios, together with the wonder that is always inherent in this sense of mystery, unleashes a bottomless spring of affectivity that sets all one's energy in motion, in accordance with the emotiveness so typical of adolescence and young adulthood. As life goes on, this emotiveness takes on a degree of density and lucidity that was previously unimaginable. These qualities show us the dignity of affinity with the divine (mystery), which characterizes the substance of our personality. Naturally, this occurs only if the "memory" of this sense of ultimate mystery becomes an exercise (or *ascesis*), since this provides the appropriate perspective from which to find a purpose worthy of life.

A method that, for some people, is starting to become their story

In the 1950s I began writing about the basic principles of a method of educating young people from about fourteen to twenty years of age, the age group I most interacted with at the time. The very same thoughts could be repeated today to the very same people, many of whom I am still in touch with, and who have now reached full adulthood. This leads me to the observation that I would find it difficult to distinguish between the basic methodological principles that apply specifically to youth, and those that should be retained as the permanent basis of a task that accompanies our entire lives. I would be tempted to say that there is no difference between the two, except for the patience it takes to attain even the most fragile, preliminary youthful response, and the humble dignity of much of the adult response. It is clear that, during youth, charisma prevails, while, during adulthood, the person's own story and tradition are determinative.

A wish and a proposal

In the closing words of a talk I gave not long ago, I told my audience (made up largely of young people): "My hope for you is that you will always be restless."[12] As I conclude these introductory thoughts, I would like to repeat this wish to my readers and briefly outline what I mean by it.

Practically speaking, if the provocation that the ideal, by its nature and function, causes in the present moment in the life of the individual were to cease, this would coincide with the death of the spirit. This provocation is the essence of the restlessness that drives human beings to penetrate into the unknown, such that we might say that the unknown is the most fascinating aspect of the Great Presence.

The provocative unknown continues to be just that, even when someone, having received grace, dares to address It as "you."

These introductory pages, in which we have become acquainted, come forth from the experience of an ecclesial movement. I would like to point out how they may offer a methodological proposal even for people who not only do not participate in that movement, but who participate in other ways of expressing Christian life, or who are Christian but do not participate in any community-based experience, and even for those who do not share the Christian vision of life at all.

I believe that the educational factors indicated by the words *reason*, *tradition*, *verification*, and *authoritative* or *provocative presence* are revealing, and that they shed light on the path for anyone who is the slightest bit "moral." I mean moral in the sense that one recognizes an ultimate destiny for one's life, to which all of existence refers, and to which everything we do (if we observe it correctly) will never measure up, but which, at the same time, somehow "saves" existence, at once so full of both beauty and wretchedness.

Chapter One

The Dynamic and Elements of the Educational Event

I. Preliminary Observations

Two preliminary observations can provide immediate insight into the ideas laid out below, and help us to better understand their contents.

The first premise

Eine Einführung in die Wirklichkeit,[1] the introduction into reality: this is what education is. The word *reality* is to the word *education* as the destination is to a journey. The destination is the meaning of all of human travels. It exists not only at the time the endeavour is completed and ends, but also at each step along the path. *Reality,* then, wholly shapes the educational motion step-by-step, in addition to being its fulfillment.

Eine Einführung in die Gesamtwirklichkeit, introduction to the total reality: this is how Jungmann explained his definition. And the word *total* here has an interesting double meaning. That is, education means developing all the structures within an individual to bring them to holistic fulfillment and, at the same time, affirming all the possibilities those structures have to connect with all of reality. In other words, the very same phenomenon brings about a totalizing effect both on the dimensions that make up the individual person and on their surrounding relationships.

Thus, every single element of the essential dynamism of the educational trajectory is undeniably marked by reality: its perspectives, its modalities, and its fabric of interconnections. Reality shapes this trajectory and dominates it – it shapes it from its origins, and it dominates it as its end. Any educational method that maintains even a modicum of loyalty to evidence must both recognize and, in some way, engage with this "reality."

We can say, without a doubt, that the more obedient an education is to this·reality, the more value it has. Obedient here means that it suggests attending to reality, following even its slightest indications, including, first of all, the original need of dependency and the patience through which we evolve.

The second premise

This pedagogical realism can be distilled in the following way: we never truly affirm reality unless we affirm the existence of its meaning.[2] Thus, the educational process is undergirded by a meaning of the total reality. The mind soaks up this meaning in the first phase of its introduction to reality. Then the adolescent mind becomes aware of it as it experiences its consistency. And the mature mind of the adult pursues it tirelessly, or else abandons it for a more radical meaning. While infancy and childhood are the period of primitive absorption in the arc of an individual's development, adolescence, starting from thirteen or fourteen years of age, is the most crucial time for determining an individual's personal physiognomy. Adolescents become aware of themselves and of the total meaning of the reality that surrounds them.

Due to educators' insensitivity to the onset of this phase, which is new and unlike childhood, or because of their inflexibility in adjusting to the new needs that arise with adolescence (which is often the result of having received an education which ignored them in its turn), the vast majority of adolescents fall into those familiar, untenable situations: either acts of rebellion that look incomprehensible at first glance, or conformist compliance lacking in any passion or convictions. The entire future physiognomy of these individuals will be compromised by the echo of these situations. This, as a result, will also compromise the future physiognomy of the world they create.

It is not our purpose here to record or describe all the issues involved in thoughtfully educating adolescents. Rather, it is to precisely delineate the fundamental framework for resolving so great and complex a set of issues; that is, to provide the essential guide-lines for an appropriate educational method.

II. Loyalty to "Tradition": The Source of the Capacity for "Certainty"

The value of this principle

If we use the word *tradition* to refer to the original *given* – the entire initial structure of values and mean-ings into which a person is born – then we must say that the first guideline for educating adolescents is to loyally adhere to this tradition.

This tradition serves as a sort of "explanatory hypothesis of reality" for the young person. No dis-covery can be made – that is, no new step may be taken, no contact with reality may be generated by the person – except through a set idea of possible meanings. This idea, whether more or less explicit, is nonetheless present and active. Fundamentally, the working hypothesis gives people certainty about the positivity of their own endeavours, without which nothing happens and nothing is achieved. This allows for the marvellous eruption of discoveries, the mar-vellous succession of steps and chain of connections that characterize the development, or education, of a being. In other words, their "*introduction* to the total reality" cannot occur without some idea of mean-ing that the individual in formation considers to be sufficiently solid, intense, and sure. Nature demands this, with an analogy that applies perfectly in every respect. Sparking this "hypothesis" is the mark of genius. Offering it to one's pupils is the humanity of the teacher. And following it like a light in the adventure of one's own journey is the first intelligence of the pupil. Genius is testifying to a vision of the world. It is always, therefore, the offering of a hypothesis of life. When education is understood in this way, the occurrence of genius finds justified expression, and genius becomes teacher. Only an era of pupils can give rise to an era of geniuses, because only people who are, first, capable of listening and understanding can later develop the personal maturity necessary to address and judge matters, until – eventually – they reach the point of being able to abandon what nourished them in the beginning.

Every single person must, inevitably, follow the path we have just described. The encounter with someone who is, for the child or young person, the bearer of what we have called an "explanatory hypothesis of reality" is not something that can be avoided. The *family* provides the first place where this occurs: the initial hypothesis is the vision of the world espoused by the parents, or the people to whom the parents delegate the responsibility of educating their child. Care for one's child, and concern for his or her formation, simply cannot exist without a (at the very least vague and confused, nearly instinctual) vision of the meaning of the world. Education consists of introducing kids to the knowledge of what is real, explaining and expounding upon this original vision.

Therefore, the inestimable distinction of this vision is that it leads young people to the certainty that things do have meaning. And here we repeat: we never truly affirm reality unless we affirm the existence of its meaning. This corresponds to the absolute need for unity that lies at the heart of every endeavour of the human mind.

It is clear that every natural dynamic must be respected in its true structure. Therefore, it is important to stress that the process of dependence must not be dumb, or *obtuse*. That is, it must not be mechanical reception on the part of the student, and inconsiderate force-feeding on the part of the teacher. The students' action should be that of following, accompanied by ever-growing awareness, while the teacher's should be that of proposing, the strength of which should rest on the reasons they are able to provide and the experiences they are able to offer. In any case, this principle cannot be denied. As always when it comes to the laws of nature, objections and problems may only be raised concerning the way it is applied.

The consequences of denying it

On the other hand, denying the principle we have just described leads to remarkably dire consequences. It is widely denied under the rationalistic and secularist contemporary worldview, which considers character to be the end product of an evolving spontaneity that requires no rule or guide other than oneself. This view posits that there is nothing upon which the person truly depends: everything extrinsic to one's own "I" is nothing more than an occasion to have reactions that are totally autonomous.

a) *In general.* This view freezes and unsettles the developing personality. A character will be built in the degree to which a person enhances their true freedom of judgment and true freedom of choice. Now, in order to judge and choose, we need a yardstick, a criterion. And if the criterion fails to affirm the original reality in which nature forms us, people will delude themselves into thinking that they have created it for themselves. In the majority of cases, however, they will actually be surrendering to a reaction or submitting to an external force, which amounts to being swept along. New phenomena, in the form of events or claims that are more stimulating to young people's instincts or inclinations, present less of a challenge to their inertia, are more violently shocking to them, or are presented in a more captivating way that will automatically prevail upon them as criteria.

In reality, the supposed autonomy of the secularist worldview actually takes the form of alienation from oneself at every instant. It amounts to constant renunciation of any true initiative, to submit to violence – a violence that does not arouse general scandal only because it is so tragically stealthy.

In the long run, this has extremely serious consequences for young people's characters. A lively mind that is made to go forward with no precise orientation will perceive this as a waste of time. This, then, generates the typical kind of uncertainty that frightens young people, whom nature puts in a position of obvious need for clear possibility. Alternatively, it confuses them, as one is confused in the face of ambiguity. In any case, it makes them impatient. This impatience comes from the fact that the indecisiveness of the offer presented to them strikes them instinctively as contradicting the essential call of things – a call to immediate acceptance. The result of all this is indifference, disaffection, and a tremendous lack of engagement with reality, which students so often display through an air of disoriented or bitterly detached scorn for any serious invitation to apply themselves.

The need to engage with reality is so global in scope that young people feel attracted to a decisive proposal even when it, in the partialness of its formulation, denies that globality. While the politicization of young people demonstrated the extent of a true need, it also showed us that this ideological hypothesis (politics), which is thought to account for all of reality, in actuality utterly reduces adolescents' need. It places young people at the mercy of the same indecisiveness and the same skeptical emptiness that are produced by an educational framework lacking in any clear interpretive hypothesis of reality.

The results are the same because the method is equally flawed. Indeed, there is no real difference between, on the one hand, presenting the various worldviews in a way that is allegedly neutral and respectful of one's supposed freedom of choice, and, on the other, offering, as an interpretation of all of reality, an ideology which, both by nature and as it turns out according to experimental evidence, cannot embrace reality in its entirety. Both methods are founded upon illusions. The first is founded upon the illusion that the human personality is characterized by an evolving spontaneity, and thus contains in itself the criteria for becoming mature. The second is founded upon the claim that it can reduce the scope of reality to a partial viewpoint. On the practical level, this attempts to fit the criterion for dealing with reality into a choice that is not actually able to contain it. The extremity of the mismatch between reality and the ideology is borne out by the angst suffered by young people who take a politicized approach, when all the baggage of personal questions concerning their own experience must be artificially and laboriously related to politics.

Only education as an introduction to the human and cosmic reality, in light of a hypothesis that is offered by a "history" or "tradition," can systematically prevent young people from taking a first step that is disoriented and dissociated precisely on account of the inconsistency or patchiness with which the "truth" is presented to them (truth being the correspondence between the young person and reality, the meaning of existence). And only this kind of education, through this prevention, can launch the young mind into its impact with reality with serenity and solidity.

Nature constructs each individual person with a specific material, in a specific situation, with a particular structure, and with distinct mannerisms, and then launches him or her into a universal comparison of everything against this initial formula. The human mind later reworks the initial given it started with through the original work of its freedom and intelligence. But only when we, first of all, unpack this given with respect can we rework it through perceptive wisdom and personal energy. Newman said that all conversions are nothing more than the deeper understanding of what you already truly wanted to begin with. Every true conversion is a deepening of pre-existing understanding. The strange notion of novelty so popular today forgets that every experience of true novelty, and of gain, therefore, is necessarily a comparison with something that remains. Otherwise it would not be novelty, but dissolution, dust.

The secularist claim is deeply deceptive, precisely because self-awareness is necessary in order to carry out a true comparative analysis. This analysis relies upon the intense development of the original given that forms the underlying bedrock of the mind. And the more aware someone is of the givens that make up their starting point, and of the internal structures they have to make use of, the more their ventures will be personal; that is, rationally "chosen."

b) *At school*. The influence of the secularist mentality is highly visible in schools.

First of all, the instruction does not bother to offer students help to effectively consider a holistic explanatory hypothesis. The predominantly analytical nature of the curriculum abandons students in the face of a panoply of heterogeneous things and contradictory solutions, leaving them, in proportion to their intelligence, bewildered, dejected, and uncertain.

This heterogeneity and contradiction are not at all remedied by the recent introduction of instructional guidelines intended to eliminate the analytical approach by patching up the most conspicuous instances of superficiality and fragmentation in the curriculum. The superficiality and fragmentation bely an underlying emptiness, which is like a disease that is only partly diagnosed and, therefore, only partly treated. The result, so typical of incomplete treatments, is that the patient shows new signs of distress, which, unfortunately, often end up simply compounding the previous ones.

We might compare students to an intelligent child who enters a room and finds a large alarm clock sitting on the table. She is clever and curious, so she picks up the clock and slowly takes it apart, piece by piece. In the end, she has fifty or a hundred pieces in front of her. She has been very good at taking apart the clock, but at this point she is confused and begins to cry. She has all the pieces, but the clock is gone; she does not have the plans that would allow her to put it back together.

Young students generally lack a guide to help them discover the comprehensive meaning of things, without which they experience a dissociation that is more or less conscious, but is always exhausting. The following words, published in a student newspaper many years ago, have surprising relevance today:

The truly negative thing about school is that it does not introduce you to humanity through the values that it handles in an all too often futile way. Although human nature is revealed in every single action of human beings, the ridiculous (or tragic?!) fact of schools is that they sweep pointlessly over millennia of human civilization, studying all the various manifestations of humans, without knowing how to reconstruct the figure of the human being itself with any degree of precision; that is, its significance within reality. Our schools are built upon an unnatural neutralism, which flattens any and all values [...]. But the blindness of our times makes it exceedingly rare that schools are ever listed among the suspects for crimes it truly commits. We accuse it of failing to form good technicians and specialized experts; we accuse it when it comes to the Latin question or to issues relating to the exam schedule for high school diplomas. But it will not be accused of failing to form true men and women, unless one of these non-men commits some vulgar and outrageous bit of "idiocy," like an act of racial intolerance.[3]

Skepticism, whether larval or full-fledged, becomes students' underlying psychic setting. It takes the form of a subtle and tremulous aura in some, or (in the most sensitive students) that of a howling gale or wild storm. In any case, it robs them completely of any capacity for passion, and they become like people walking on sand, their energy and efforts sapped by the unstable terrain. People often complain that young people do not build anything: but what should they be building, and on what ground? As one boy said to a group of fellow high school students: "They make us memorize a million things, but they don't help us understand what they mean at all. So it looks to us like there's no reason why we should learn them in the first place."

When it comes to Christian teachers, the fact that no hypothesis is offered as the holistic explanatory criterion even implies that the figure of Christ, as the keystone of all reality, is missing. *Mundus per ipsum factus est, et mundus eum non cognovit* (the world came to be through him, but the world did not know him).[4] And this "world" could easily include Christian educators!

This may bring to mind the line, so often recited by advocates of secular schooling, that in order for children to be free, they must formulate an individual comprehensive conception of things by themselves. Supposedly they are perfectly capable of doing so when they are indiscriminately, spontaneously introduced to all the various theories. The different ideological viewpoints of the various teachers (so the theory goes) provide the ideal conditions to allow for the "auto-formation" of broad minds. But here life experience confirms, with utmost clarity, what our nature suggests from the beginning. Experience teaches us that when young people are faced prematurely with conflicting ideas about fundamental questions of the interpretation of life, this disorients them rather than orienting them: a less than reassuring result for an education. And it is bitter to hear that this disorientation is intentionally provoked on purely methodological grounds, and even considered to be a crucial rite of passage, because people do not realize (or do not want to recognize) that simply being tossed into the fray inevitably produces skepticism in a young person. This happens above all when *young people, without having been prepared for it, feel that they are being contradicted with respect to the fundamental and secure ideas that they received from their earlier education.* When this happens, an act of violence is committed against them, in the truest sense of the word, and we know from humanity's long memory that violence builds nothing, and leaves only ruins in its wake.

Moreover, skepticism is absolutely not a rite of passage. It molds a deep-seated state of mind that will continue to be a deciding factor in the way a person looks at life, and in the reasons that motivate their decisions about it. Life forces us to make judgments and choices. Young people feel the urgent need to do this, and they will make their judgments and their choices. But once they have lost their healthy natural adherence to objective criteria, which they had from their origins, they will make judgments and choices by abandoning themselves to rigid preconceptions, dictated by their own idiosyncrasies or instinctive leanings, or else by referring to criteria based on narrow worldviews, or worldviews drawn from one specific source. Skepticism is a basic mind-set that endures, and the way people move beyond it in practice is by crossing into fanaticism. That is, they cross over into the uncompromising affirmation of one-sidedness. This same situation applies to students who keep their previous religious and moral views even after their unprepared passage through this violent conflict. This is because, to avoid giving up their views, they cling to them, practically barricading themselves into a fortress of prudence or of fear, which, in any case, is totally without openness toward what they consider to be a hostile environment. Other young people, equally unprepared for the clash, react by turning their backs in an uncritical rejection of all the religious instruction they ever received, without ever seriously examining it, giving in to the fierce urge to shake it off.

As absurd as it may seem, it appears that the skepticism that the "neutral" schooling model tends to generate produces only two outcomes: fanaticism and bigotry (fanaticism for, bigotry against); or else indifference and detachment.

Perhaps nothing can better explain the natural brilliance of schools with an explicit ideology. As a rule, this is the only kind of school able to create truly free spirits and truly open minds. Precisely because they educate students in the affirmation of a single criterion, these institutions can create in young people an intense interest in building comparisons with other ideologies, as well as a sincere and sympathetic openness toward them. Lively openness and true *sympathy* (or appreciation) are only possible when they come from a (sometimes unwitting) sense of universal security. With them, a student may ask, "If the criterion you suggest is true, in what way, and why do the other ideologies fail to allow for it?" And "If the approach you propose is right, in what way, and why do others act differently?" These are questions that would lose their way in the mind of a skeptic, or would be cut short in the mind of a fanatic, but they become a passionate and careful adventure of inquiry in a person educated to know that an answer to them exists.

c) *In the family*. Similar observations can be made about the educational relationship between adolescents and their families.

It is not right that parents are afraid (perhaps mostly after their children reach fourteen or fifteen years of age, but increasingly even beforehand) to propose fundamental ideas to their children with conviction. It is equally wrongheaded for parents to refrain from proposing them at all because of a misinterpretation of freedom, which profoundly conflicts with their children's need to have a precise hypothesis in their lives. Indifference at home very often becomes, in the hearts of young people, the root of a skepticism that is even more resistant to removal than the negative influence of neutral schools. Loyalty to the origin must, first of all, be loyalty to parents. This overlaps with being loyal to oneself, given that parents are, in fact, the origin of their children, and, for this reason, most properly deserve the name of "genitors," parents. Giving a child life would count for nothing if parents failed to tirelessly help their children to recognize the total meaning of that life.

The educational genius of the family is particularly evident in the people parents choose to collaborate with in the work of educating their children. It is somewhat shocking to witness the nearly universal spectacle of families who, after having spent years giving their children precise foundational ideas, do not bother to ensure that they may then verify these ideas in adolescence. Thus, they permit (with a lack of awareness that, for all its innocence, is no less ruinous) "neutral" and secularist education to accomplish its masterpiece of destruction and imbalance in the minds of their children. It is important to stress here, once again, that this is not a matter of defending certain values that are threatened by secularist schools. Rather, the prevailing issue is that of saving people's mental integrity, of recognizing and supporting the vital energy of young people, to engage with whatever view of life was instilled in them by their families.

I would conclude this point with the following thought: Loyalty to the given, to the tradition from which the young person's mind originates, is the backbone of every responsible education. First of all, it lays the foundation for a sense of dependence, without which we violate and manipulate reality through presumptuousness, alter it through fantasy, or empty it through delusion. Second, it accustoms us to facing reality with the certainty that a solution exists. Without this, our very capacity to discover and energy to create relationships with things wither away.

III. Authority: The Existentiality of a Proposal

The points of tradition who are most aware are the people who are ultimately responsible for an adolescent's education. They are the "place of the hypothesis" for that adolescent. This is the authentic idea of *authority* (from *auctoritas*, "what makes one grow").

The experience of authority begins within us as the encounter with a person rich in knowledge of reality. This person strikes us as enlightening, and generates in us a sense of novelty, wonder, and respect. In this person is an unavoidable attractiveness, and in us an inevitable subjugation. Indeed, the experience of authority reminds us, more or less clearly, of our poverty and limitation. This leads us to follow and to make ourselves "disciples" of that person. But if adults recognize and choose an authority through a comparison that engages their mature responsibility, in younger people the choice is fixed by the nature of the individual's "originating reality." The genuine revelation of life and genuine truth lie in the development of our dependence upon this "authoritative" reality. It follows that authority is the concrete expression of the working hypothesis. Authority serves as the criterion of my experimentation of the values given to me by tradition, and it is the expression of the union in which my life originates. In a certain sense, authority is my truest "I." But today it frequently happens that an authority is perceived as something external that is "added on" to the individual. The authority remains external to the person's mind, even if the person may devotedly accept the authority as a limit.

The educational function of a true authority takes the shape of a "function of consistency (or coherence)." The authority acts as a constant reminder of ultimate values and call for the mind to engage with them, a permanent criterion for judging all of reality, and a solid protection of the link (which is always new) between the shifting attitude of the young person and the total, ultimate meaning of reality.

From the experience of authority comes the experience of consistency, or coherence. Consistency is efficient stability over time, or continuity of life. In a patiently evolving phenomenon such as the "introduction to total reality," consistency is an indispensible element. An original certainty that is incapable of continuing to re-propose itself through the consistency of its evolution over time will end up being perceived as abstract. It will become a given that is passively borne but never actively examined. Without the company of a true authority, any "hypothesis" will remain just that, its only transformation being crystallization over time; or, alternatively, every later initiative will wipe out the original hypothesis. On the contrary, consistency, if it is the constant presence of a total meaning of reality, beyond the individual's momentary "tastes" or capricious "opinions," is a powerful education in the dependent nature of the real.

Parents are, first and foremost, authorities, whether they are aware of it or not. Their function is that of origination, and, for this reason, it is also one of inclusion in a particular way of understanding reality, in a particular stream of thought and of civilization. The authoritativeness of parents, which is inevitable, is a fact, a responsibility. They themselves may fail to recognize this fact, but it persists. In the life of an adolescent, parents represent the permanent consistency of the origin with itself, the constant dependence upon a total meaning of reality, which precedes the individual person's approval, and which exceeds the scope of that approval.

In Christianity, this natural function of providing a constant and consistent reference to everything's ultimate meaning is supremely appreciated by the Church (the "mother" of all believers). In its broadest and most comprehensive capacity, the Church represents the constant source of the hypothesis within which Christian parents generate their children. In Christianity, *parents* and *Church* are the ultimate guarantee of the consistency necessary for any education.

Schools are also clearly authorities, to the extent that they continue and further develop the education provided by families. It is strange that, in the allegedly perfect kind of school, the teaching could almost be done by a tape player. The most typically human thing about the teacher-pupil relationship is removed: the specifically human contribution, the genius of the master. In an agnostic or "neutral" school, the absence of any proffered meaning makes the teacher no longer a "master," and leads students to vaunt themselves as their own masters and to codify their contingent impressions and reactions with that widespread presumptuousness brimming with impertinence and closed-minded prejudices which so often today destroy the candor and openness of youth.

The impossibility and absurdity of such a system is compounded by presenting young people with the widest and most varied possible range of different authorities. Supposedly juxtaposing all of them will lead students to spontaneously choose the best one and gain maturity of judgment. I will not restate the reasons (laid out above) why it seems to me that this is the counter-educational method *par excellence*.

Here I will only add that such a system eliminates the consistency of education. In so doing, it makes authority useless; that is, it makes nature useless (the adolescent's development is, literally, "denatured"). It stamps out the evolutionary nature and homogeneity that are necessary elements of the educational phenomenon, just as they are necessary for every other phenomenon of human life. It is a system that generates only irrationality and anarchy.

IV. Personal Verification of the Educational Hypothesis

The necessity thereof

In order to adequately respond to the educational needs of adolescence, it is not enough to propose a meaning of the world in clear terms. Nor is it enough for the person making the proposal to have a certain intensity of real authority. Rather, one must cultivate a personal *engagement on the part of the young person with his or her own origins*. They must verify what tradition has offered them, and this may only be done *on their own initiative*, and no one else's.

One of the most important characteristics of a personality is the "force of *conviction*." A personality's creative flow, its constructive contribution, depends on this force for continuity and strength. Now, conviction comes from the experience of finding that an idea we have embraced or received is vitally linked with our own needs and projects. Conviction arises as a verification, in which the initial idea or vision serves as the keystone for all other encounters. The initial idea is deeply related to the events of our life, and, therefore, sheds a resolving light on our experiences. Our entire personal reality is positioned in correspondence with that original idea. At first, it serves as an unconscious initial hypothesis, and then, as its validity is experienced little by little over time, it gains the devotion of our whole being.

The supreme concern of true education, precisely because it resolutely proposes a certain vision of things, is that adolescents be educated to carry out a constant comparison not only between this vision and other people's views, but also and above all between whatever happens to them and the idea that is offered to them (*tràdita*, "passed on"). The need for this personal experimentation is urgent, and this implies that the educator must tirelessly solicit adolescents' personal "responsibility," because once the educator proposes the idea and offers cooperation, only conscious engagement on the part of the individual student can concretize the value of the proposal and uncover its existential validity.

Inviting students to take personal responsibility is very different from reminding them in an abstract (academic) way of this or that principle. And it is even more different from inciting them, more or less subtly, to dispense with all traditions. Rather, the invitation to personal responsibility must become an educational method. It is not enough for young people to feel that the announcement of the ideal is present to them. They must make themselves present to the ideal value, "by doing it." The word that the educator constantly announces – sometimes explicitly, sometimes implicitly – becomes a well thought-out inspiration for living, a knowledgeable paradigm for action. *Veritatem facientes in caritate* (speaking the truth in love).[5]

Education today is lacking due to its rationalistic framework, which neglects the important fact that existential engagement is a necessary condition for one to have a genuine experience of truth, and, therefore, to have a conviction. You cannot understand reality if you are not in reality. St. Thomas Aquinas wrote: *In hoc enim aliquis percipit se animam habere et vivere et esse, quod percipit se sentire et intelligere et alia huiusmodi opera vitae exercere.*[6] We understand that we *are* because we *act*. The more we engage with our vital energy, the more we realize what we are.

Here we can see how present-day educators often fall into errors of superficiality and abstraction.

Educating is all too often taken to mean simply explaining concepts. But after the explanations are laid out, there is still a great deal to do because they are abstract and extraneous. They are still mere sounds and words. Our energy, our freedom must be engaged. This energy can make me apply my entire being to both the idea and the practical framework of intelligence. At first, our energy will seem merely to join the two things together from the outside, but if it bears on, the proposed idea will gradually become "flesh and blood."

Even the most brilliant piece of evidence will never become conviction if the "I" does not become acquainted with the object, if it does not open itself up to the object with care and patience, does not give it time, does not live with it; if it does not love it, in short. Contemporary rationalism forgets and denies the basic dependency of the self. It forgets or denies the great, original surprise that is evidence. One ninth grader, after a debate, defined evidence in this way: becoming aware of an unavoidable presence. Contemporary rationalism forgets or denies that to live is to share this presence, and that, for this reason, there is a companionship that must be accepted, faithfully and intensely, if we wish to live intelligently.

The current mentality unfortunately teaches young people to follow things only up to a point that they already find acceptable, and no more. Thus, this evidentiary "presence" is treated as a basis for affirming one's own concerns and preconceptions, and not as something to be faithfully followed through and through. Then, when the presence does not correspond to predetermined concerns, a rapid fire of "buts" and "ifs" often provides cover for closed-mindedness and a lack of genuine love for truth and goodness. This accounts for that widespread fear, that strange incapacity of young people to affirm being. This fear of affirming being comes directly from a lack of engagement with being, whether it translates into the indifference that characterizes most people's lives, or expresses itself in the "drunkard's terror" described by the poet Montale.[7] Let us try to imagine just how intense and solid our adherence to existence must be (I say *existence* and not an interpretation thereof) in order to follow the complete voice of reality in its analogic call, to the point of reaching personal values, to the point of reaching God! It is natural for kids to halt immediately, before they even start, unless they are helped to adhere to existence sincerely. In the same student newspaper quoted above, the student wrote:

> Is it possible to prescribe a treatment after so bleak a diagnosis? Maybe so: the only educational medium that can make us discover man's true humanity, the path man must take in order to be fulfilled without equivocation, is a courteous attention (instinctive, we might say) to what is positive, in whatever form it appears: the pages of a book, the voice of a teacher, or the surpassing concreteness of a loving gesture. The bitter thing about this situation today is that we must walk

the path toward positivity alone, and our instinctive love for it is not always able to sustain us to the point of reaching our goal.[8]

The fundamental point here is in line with the words of Seneca:

I have mentioned all this in order to show you how zealous neophytes are with regard to their first impulses towards the highest ideals, provided that some one does his part in exhorting them and in kindling their ardour. There are indeed mistakes made, [... including] mistakes made by the pupils, who come to their teachers to develop, not their souls, but their wits. Thus the study of [philosophy] has become the study of words [and what was once wisdom has become what we now call science].[9]

To summarize this we would have to say that, psychologically, conviction arises from a discovery that is proposed by our intelligence as a comprehensive hypothesis, but which is verified by love through dedication to existence. For this reason, in order to help bring about conviction, an education must, on the one hand, clearly and decisively propose a comprehensive meaning of things and, on the other, tirelessly push adolescents to compare every encounter they have with that criterion. That is, they must be pushed to apply themselves to personal experience, to a process of existential verification.

Let us try to think of how enormously important all of this must be for religious conviction. We can briefly list the shortcomings so often found at the very heart of our religious education. First of all, the absence of Christ from the encounter with all things – with *all* things. And perhaps His profound relevance is not even proposed at all! In this case, the pupil prefers to indulge in intellectual daydreaming rather than accept the mystery. Second, the desire to understand something before seriously taking it on. Sadly this error is extremely widespread and commonly nurtured. Fortunately for us, time exists, which makes us grow old. The goodness of God exists, which tosses us into unexpected encounters. And nature exists, which shatters indifference and brings us back to deeper perspectives. Without these, our desire to engage only after understanding would mean never engaging at all. Third, the negligent way of dealing with the change people undergo at a certain age, when the ideas they have received, the gestures they have devotedly repeated, and their obedient humility must all become like a hypothesis that is tested in the new experiences that they face alone as individuals. If, for the four or five years after young people reach the age of fourteen, they are not persistently and systematically helped to see the connection between the given ("the tradition") and life, then their new experiences will lay the groundwork for them to adopt one of the three attitudes that are the enemies of Christianity: indifference, traditionalism, or hostility. Indifference makes them perceive everything that does not enter into direct contact with experience as abstract. Traditionalism is where the most good-hearted and the least lively of people rigidly hole themselves up in order to avoid seeing what is outside and in order to avoid feeling that their faith is being disturbed. And hostility arises because an abstract God is certainly an enemy, of which we can say, at the very least, that he wastes our time.

The pivotal method for preventing people of a certain age from falling into these attitudes is to assist them as they experimentally test what has been given them, which must be placed in comparison with every thing (this "every" is important in the comparison, since otherwise people grow one-sided and rigidly set in their ideas).

The conditions thereof

If *all* the needs of a young person's humanity and *all* the encounters that he or she experiences must be considered in comparison with the educational hypothesis, then certain conditions must be met.

a) The first condition necessary for young people to verify their hypothesis is that they be helped to seriously grapple with something *in their environment* in keeping with an ideal, because the fabric of inner and outer experiences of the young person draws inspiration, promptings, and nourishment from within the environment. Therefore, it is, above all, through engaging with the environment that the validity of the education they have received will become clear. Nothing is more deleterious, debilitating, and exasperating in the long term for an adolescent than feeling that they are not aided in a human way to face their environment with the necessary degree of clarity and decisiveness.

Families and schools have formative responsibilities in this regard that are so laden with consequences for young people's convictions that their massive and often unconscious negligence is nearly inconceivable. Never before has the environment, understood as mental climate and lifestyle, had tools at its disposal that are so despotically invasive of minds. Today, more than ever before, the environment, in all its expressive forms, is the sovereign educator, or dis-educator. For this reason, the crisis may be understood, first of all, as a lack of awareness that makes educators themselves the (perhaps unwitting) accomplices of the shortcomings in the environment. Secondly, the crisis may be understood as a lack of vitality in the educational attitude, which fails to help students resist with sufficient energy the negativity of the environment. This is because the educational approach posts educators along rigidly traditional and formalistic lines instead of leading them to renew the eternal redeeming Word in the spirit of the new struggle.

This issue has particular importance in the lives of students, because the figure of the educator (in the strictest meaning of the word, the teacher) exists in a fabric of insinuating and prompting presences that are more effective beyond compare than in any other field. Each instance of uncertainty in the face of the environment on the part of the educator translates into an interior surrender on the part of the young person, into a non-verification of the ideal.

b) Real dependency upon a total meaning of things demands, as a matter of psychology, that young people not carry out their verification in the environment in a solitary (and, therefore, independent or "abstract") way. An adolescent needs to live out his or her way of facing all of reality in a *communal* way.

Few words are so often repeated as *community*, and few concepts are so poorly lived out and, above all, so little understood. Community is the profound unity that arises from the shared living brought about by a common structure. In our dedication to organization, we tend to confuse associations with community. We believe that we can make a community in the form of a convergence from the outside, in the form of an agreement to do some particular thing. Community, precisely because it is essential shared living, is an interior dimension, at the origin of our thoughts and our actions. Otherwise it is not community, but calculation. Community is a way of understanding things, a way of facing the question of being, or that of studying history, or that of love. A community, in short, is a way of approaching everything.

In every truly educational human endeavour, a communal dimension is present. Suffice it to think of the community that is the most originating and decisive for education: the family. No great educational genius has ever acted without immediately generating community. The sense of universality inevitably generates the sense of community. A hypothesis of a total meaning that is truly lived out can only present itself in the form of community.

In Catholicism, this "ontological" structure of the search for truth is actually a condition for salvation, the inexhaustible presence of Meaning among humankind. The classic function of "authority" itself is to generate community (*plantatio Ecclesiae*, the plant of the Church).

This calls to mind the common educational framework that may well be "religious," but that is individualistic, inward-looking, or coldly rationalistic, both at home and in other settings. It is a framework incapable of forming truly open personalities, who intimately understand the values they claim to uphold. Because a value may be verified only on the basis of its ability to sustain relationships, and first of all relationships with other people, all other people.

Likewise, "neutral" schooling, with its lack of concern for providing a unified ideological vision, is incapable of generating real communities, since it deprives young people of a capital structure for their own personal search (how true the maxim that says that to deny one facet of humanity is to contradict it in its totality).

Systematic validation of the communitarian responsibility of young people is, therefore, an indispensable pedagogical guideline for any educational place that is engaged at the ideological level and an all-inclusive tool for bringing about illuminated conviction in students.

c) Another condition necessary for an educational process of verification, which is, to some extent, the consequence of the other two, is the use of free time. Free time is the space in which young people most transparently choose for themselves. Through the use of free time, an adolescent can collect evidence of his or her own "share" in the educational hypothesis. Free time is the point at which an idea most easily transitions from "duty," to "fascination," to the purely voluntary initiative of the adolescent, to a responsibility that is knowledgeably and generously taken on. An education incapable of fascinating young people in their free time (or, worse, an education that reduces itself to hoping it will be able to lure young people to the ideal, who knows how, by endorsing a way of using free time that does not give primary importance to courageous engagement with the ideal itself) is certainly too narrow, and, humanly speaking, inadequate. This is the case with a great deal of intellectualized catechesis, which tends to consider kids' free time to be time in which, having left behind instruction about ideals, the best we can hope for is that they don't misbehave. Others, who are more sensitive to kids' humanity, hope to be able to extract some engagement with values from free time that is primarily about amusement.

On the contrary, we must directly face young people, with an honest and serious proposal for how they may apply themselves to the values, precisely during the times that are totally under their control. Adolescents immediately understand what is being asked of them, and they either stay or leave. If they stay, the task of educating them takes on a serious outline. By engaging with the ideal in their free time, young people learn to pursue their hypothesis even at other times, when the pressures of necessity or contingent influences make doing so more difficult.

Any form of demanding impatience on the part of educators (be they at school or at home) concerning this step is unjustified. Such impatience betrays an abstract approach and a lack of understanding of the sure but gradual evolution of the educational phenomenon. It would be inappropriate to call upon a person who is already living out an ideal in free time, to take on their academic, family, or other "duties" as though these priorities were somehow pitted against their dedication to the ideal in free time. Free time is most likely to be the authentic space for young people's personalities, and educators must look there, first of all, as the appropriate place for asking them to apply themselves personally and generously to the ideal.

The "dimensions" thereof

One last matter we might address is this: how can we elicit the energy, how can we provoke the level of engagement necessary to carry out a verification, the only thing that may give rise to conviction?

Here it is necessary to search for those instances that are not so much philosophical explanations or ideological clarifications, but which may be compared, in human life, to basic biological life needs. Like biological life, the human and Christian mind has its basic needs. If the Christian call, for example, no longer arouses the engagement we described, couldn't it be that the way the call is issued utterly lacks the capacity to "touch" the essential structures of the mind with those "motives" that (as the root of the word suggests) are able to "move"? Couldn't it be that the way the call is issued does not correspond to the "dimensions" of the spirit; that is, to those structural needs that, once they are evoked, set all the person's energy in motion?

If we overemphasize our insistence on "willpower," we can easily fall into a misunderstanding. The misunderstanding comes about when the insistence on willpower traps the mind at the level of analysis, isolating individual duties or specific values from the total context (the total context being the "ideal"), or else focuses all the attention on the (perhaps scrupulous) observation of minor issues, feelings, moods, attempts, efforts, and so on. There we run the serious risk of forgetting that human beings will only resign themselves to the particular if that particular seems to them to be the fulfillment of a universal. Only what is great, only what is total, only what is compendious can enliven human energy to face what is minute and mundane. Ascesis itself wearies us if it is not carried out with full awareness of a spacious end, one that is truly worthy of human horizons.

It is crucial to cast young people "outside themselves" toward compendious and definitive horizons. Pope Pius XII said that the universal views of the Church are the ordinary instructions of Christians.[10] We refer to these total contexts, these "ideals," as "dimensions." Each one of them constitutes an aspect of that openness toward the total horizon that is proper to every human action.

These dimensions of the adolescent spirit (for the sake of which alone may we correctly address adolescents with an adequate call to apply themselves) may be briefly defined in the following way:

a) The need for a total explanation of reality (the cultural dimension in its most complete sense). There can only be one reason to dedicate oneself to verifying the educational hypothesis: that it proposes itself as a total explanation of everything – as the ultimate meaning of life, the world, and history. Any form of skepticism or encyclopedism which says that culture is a mere mishmash of materials incapable of providing a vital explanation for every page of reality, and every resulting fideism that places religion and faith outside of "culture" so defined, considering them incapable of accounting for every reality or issue that emerges, will rightly leave the young person cold, if not hostile.

b) The need for absolute radicalness in love (the dimension of charity in its most genuine sense). Loving is, first of all, a way of understanding oneself: understanding oneself as ontologically connected to the whole. The same gesture that creates me creates everything. Thus, everything is a part of my existence. Christianity mysteriously accounts for this fact: the origin of being, God, is shared life (Trinity).

Love, therefore, is not primarily a "feeling." It is not a matter of "taste," nor is it any form of "giving" that is not giving oneself. It is understanding oneself and accepting oneself as union. This must be perfectly clear in the call we put out to young people. They must be called to total purity of motives. The sentimental approach that is so fashionable in trying to appeal to young people today will be perceived by them as artificial, inessential, non-motive.

c) The need for a totality of horizons, to which their humanity is called to adhere (the missionary dimension). That the measure of love is to love without measure is not only a famous expression but also a clear axiom. *Caritas* (love, or charity) is a law without borders. It is universal, that is, catholic. Under this law, putting limits on love is not to limit it, but to destroy it. We might reflect on the fact that the Christian call is, first and foremost, to conquer the world, in the gospel sense. It is the Kingdom. Having a sense of the Kingdom means having a missionary sense. We must live for the universe, for all of humanity. To limit the scope of the potential sharing offered to us by existence is to deny ourselves, is *sin* (that is, a *deficiency*, from the Latin root meaning "to lack" something). This brings to mind the words of the Lord when he said, "everyone who commits sin is a slave of sin."[11] Indeed, to limit one's openness to to union is to seek to impose one's own measures upon the profound law of being. It is to confuse love with calculation, to conflate sharing and attempting domination. Unlimitedness is the only possible answer to the thirst that adults remain prey to in spite of themselves, and that young people experience as an urgent and present sense of need.

V. Risk: A Necessity for Freedom

The purpose of education is to form a new human being. For this reason, the active factors of an education must incline toward ensuring that students increasingly act and face the environment of their own accord. Therefore, it is important, on the one hand, to put students in increasing contact with all the various factors that make up the environment and, on the other hand, to give them increasing responsibility to choose. This should follow an evolutionary trajectory established by the awareness that adolescents must be capable of "doing it themselves" in the face of anything.

The more an adolescent approaches adulthood, the more we should use the educational method of guiding him or her toward a personal and increasingly independent encounter with the entire surrounding reality. Here the educator's balanced moderation takes on its ultimate importance. Indeed, the evolution of the adolescent's independence is a "risk" for the intelligence and heart – and also for the egotism – of the educator. At the same time, it is precisely through the risk of their impact with reality that personalities are generated within young people, in their relationship with all things. In other words, it is thus that their freedom "becomes."

The appeal to tradition may be formulated in various ways, but it must be quite clear that the true concept of tradition is that of representing values to be rediscovered in new experiences. If history and existence are vehicles of values to be rediscovered in new experiences, who must make the discovery? The parent? The teacher? No, that would be traditionalism. It is the young person who must have the experience, because this is how his or her freedom will come to be.

Above all else, educators must bear in mind this love for freedom to the point of risk.

> [Only] cowards want to know the statistical probability of victory on the morning of battle. The strong and the dedicated do not ordinarily ask how long or how hard, but rather how and where they must fight. All they need to know is in what place, by which way, and to what end. And then they hope, and work, and fight, and suffer there until the end of the day, leaving the accomplishments to God.[12]

To God, to the mystery of Being, to that Dimension that made us, and that exceeds us on all sides and cannot be measured by us – it is to This that the educator's love must entrust the increasingly broad expanse of the unforeseeable paths opened up by the freedom of the new human being in its dialogue with the universe. In the work of education we must always keep in mind that the more human an endeavour is, the more its countenance will take the shape of a humble attempt, illuminated by hope for a gracious encounter with a power and an order that are not within our ability to achieve.

A totally "independentalist" education leaves young people prey to their instinctiveness and whims, and effectively lacking in an evolutionary criterion. But an education that is dominated by fear about adolescents' confrontation with the world aims only to shelter them from the shock, and turns them into beings that may be incapable of having personality in relating to reality, or that may be defiant nearly to the point of becoming deranged. It is painfully clear that this is the case for many educators (families and schools) whose supreme ideal seems to be that of taking absolutely no risks. But the educational method with the greatest capacity for good is not the one that flees from reality in order to affirm what is good separately, but rather the one that lives by advocating for the triumph of the good in the world. "In the world" means in relationship with the whole of reality, a "risky" relationship, if you want to call it that, although it would be better to say "engaging." To separate adolescents from the world, or even just not help and guide them in their impact with the world, is to cause, in the intelligent minds of certain adolescents, the bitter discovery that a sufficient instruction for the victory of good over evil does not exist.

It is certainly necessary that education be knowledgeable and courageous concerning its implications. Basing the teaching on an ideology, without helping young people to freely engage, concretely and practically, with that ideology, will produce cultural curiosity (if the ideology is proposed well), and will leave behind only reasoned respect. In most students' lives this will translate into sentimental traditionalism, which their respect will serve only to buttress, but not to build up into conviction. The true source of faithfulness and of knowledgeable devotion to the hypothesis proposed and the person who proposes it is an education that accepts, with vigilance, the risk of the young person's freedom. The figure of the "teacher," due precisely to this discretion and respect, retreats, in a certain true sense, behind the dominating form of the One Truth that is his or her inspiration. The teaching and instruction become a gift of bearing witness, and this is exactly why they become inscribed in the memory of the pupil with acute and sincere sympathy, independent (at the deepest level) from the teacher's personal gifts. Because of this we have an ineradicable gratitude toward and bond with the teacher, and yet a conviction that is independent from him or her.

VI. Conclusion

One could say, in summary, that in the educational time span of adolescence, the "age of verification," the broad methodological guidelines to adhere to are as follows. First, the specific provision of a hypothesis of the total meaning of reality (this is the offering of "tradition"): the necessary condition for certainty for adolescents. Second, the presence of a clear and real authority, which is the locus, or "place," of this hypothesis: the necessary condition for consistency in the educational phenomenon. Third, inviting adolescents to personally apply themselves to verify the hypothesis in all their experience: the necessary condition for forming a true conviction. Fourth, acceptance of the growing, measured risk of the adolescents' independent comparison between the hypothesis and the reality in their mind: the necessary condition for attaining maturity of freedom.

At the conclusion of the educational process, the fundamental guidelines of which we have attempted to examine here, adolescents plunge into the mature phase of youth. By this time families and schools must have completed the essence of their formative task; they must have put the young person in the condition to journey forward on his or her own energy. Slowly, in a process that only the most carefully brilliant of educators will have been capable of overseeing and setting up without coercion and delays, the educator becomes increasingly detached from the pupil, encouraging personal engagement and judgment more and more. The educator has introduced the pupil into the total reality, imparting a lively sense of dependence upon that reality and of its ultimate meaning. Now it falls to the young person to continue on with the enquiry, not skeptically, but firmly convinced that things are positive and that an explanation for them exists. Have the educators not, perhaps, completed their task at this point? Should the young adult, now able to face the surrounding world alone, perhaps isolate herself in the conviction that she need have nothing more to do with anyone else? Obviously not. On the contrary, this is the start of a new journey, and it is precisely its newness that justifies an even greater bond. Now the educator and the educatee are two people; they are two among the people. This is the time of that mature and strong companionship that binds together people who live a common experience of the world, who encounter the call of being in every instant of their journey. It is the time in which they work together, side by side, toward a destiny that unites us all.

Here the "introduction" to the total reality reveals its ultimate value: that of education carried out by the most generous and brilliant people in order to introduce a young person to another, more perfect, and expanding education. In this new phase, *unus est Magister vester*[13] (you have but one Master), the mystery of Being itself, to which your adolescence has made you marvellously and knowledgeably devoted. Then you will have the otherwise unattainable miracle of a life, which, as it passes, advances in youth, in "educability," and in "wonder" and being moved by things; of a creative energy that grows exponentially, without unravelling or wearing down, but adhering with utmost care to all the possibilities produced by existence. In short, it is a time that is open to invasion by the power of the eternal, and that comes to be indefatigably fertilized by it.

Chapter Two

Crisis and Dialogue

I. The Critical Step

"Crisis" and "critique" are not the same as doubt and denial

When we think about a "new society," one grave danger would be to imagine it as something totally new, where "new" is understood as "different," and the future is understood as the elimination of the past. The word *crisis* is useful precisely in order to work against this grave danger, which looms large as a temptation for young people and as a convenient tool for too many adults.

The word *crisis* (from the Greek *krino*, "to test or sift") is ordinarily and unfortunately interpreted, in today's mindset, as being doubtful and negative, as though crisis and critique necessarily implied denial. Thus, in practice, critique is raised only for the purpose of scandalizing, always on the lookout for something to impugn, something to object to. This is clearly a short-sighted (or petty!) concept of crisis and critique.

On the contrary, critique is, first of all, the expression of the human genius that is in all of us — a genius that strains to discover being, to discover values. It suffices to add even the slightest bit of sincerity; it suffices to add a realistic balance; and the affirmation of the discovered values will also clearly suggest their limitations.

The word *crisis* is closely related to another word, the word *problem*. Not *doubt*, but *problem*, the Greek etymology of which indicates the basic attitude a young person needs to have in order to build a new society: it means to hold something before your eyes. Each of us is born with a set of endowments, which can be summarized in a magnificent word (and etymology reveals the full beauty of this word, too): *tradition*.

All of us used not to exist. Therefore, each of us is formulated from antecedents, from a package of things that constitute us, that shape us. The word *problem* refers to this phenomenon, which is crucial for true novelty in an individual life and in the life of the human cosmos. Tradition, the endowment with which life enriches us at birth and during our early development, must be lifted before our eyes so that the individual, to the extent that he or she is alive, intelligent, may sift and test (*krinei*). Tradition must "become crisis." Tradition must become a problem. Thus, crisis means becoming aware of the reality from which we feel we were made.

Therefore this is, first of all, a matter of taking the past seriously, where the word *past* indicates the starting point from which we were made to face the reality in which we find ourselves. This is the first condition for self-awareness and the first condition for a critical entrance into the world and reality, for the very reason that the condition for a critical entrance is that we be aware of the tools, of the structures through which we will, little by little, have life's encounters.

Faithfulness and freedom vis-à-vis tradition

The more we live, the more we are perceptive and lively, and the more we have intelligence and sensibility, the more our life will be interwoven with encounters. Every encounter offers a proposal of statements, persons, things, or events. In this immense chorus of proposals, which make up the fabric of our existence, human beings are, by nature, driven to "compare." They are, by nature, driven to compare every individual proposal with that complex of evidence, needs, and original structures that make up their being. In this comparison, if a proposal that is made to me appears as the elicitor of my authentic needs, the validator of my possibilities, then I immediately feel sympathy for the proposal, and I approve it.

St. Augustine spoke of a *delectatio victrix*[1] (conquering delight) in human beings. And the psychological dynamic he was referring to may be considered the inspiration for St. Thomas Aquinas' definition of truth: *adaequatio rei et intellectus* (the adequation of the intellect and the thing). That is, he defined it as a near-overlap between the proposal and what I am aware of as the structure of my nature. Let us recall the point above about critique as positivity, not as destruction but as ability to understand, not as crassness but as intelligence – as ready openness to recognizing a correspondence, not despairing of what we find, but rejoicing in what we find (because we live on what we find, and it is death to fixate on what we have not yet found). It is important to keep this point in mind above all when it comes to tradition. Indeed, the role of "crisis" is important in the story of an adolescent, as a phenomenon that brings him or her to collaborate in the construction of a new society, *to the degree to which it becomes a discovery of the meaning of history*.

This may sound like a paradox, but in order to truly build a new society it is necessary, first of all, to take the old one seriously, to take one's tradition seriously. But taking tradition seriously, taking one's own past seriously, means engaging with it in the ways it itself entails. This is how we may detect the values it contains and reject whatever is not a value, and discover any correspondence it has with what we are, freeing ourselves from any parts that only corresponded to the circumstances of an earlier time period and no longer apply to ours. Faithfulness and freedom are the two conditions without which history has no meaning, because history is a permanency that moves in constantly new versions.

And without permanence, newness cannot exist, leaving only the constant frustration of everything.

What will exist is the basic desperation of the sensibility of contemporary people – their raging and relent-
less attempt to solve all the anxiety of their minds by
turning themselves into a totally different creation.
And the creation of an entirely different human thing
is an insane exaggeration, a maniacal image.

Applying ourselves to the Christian tradition

The starting point of this crisis, of this engagement
with tradition from which the future may arise, is
our situation. We have been made to live within the
ambit of a proposal that is, by nature, the grand-
est proposal imaginable. There are some proposals
which, by their very nature, demand a response. Saying "yes" or "no" to them is unavoidable; sharing in
them or raging against them is inevitable. And there
is no proposal more serious than this one, none more
colossal or more invasive than this: a man who says,
"I am God."

This man continues on through history, invading
geography and time until he reaches me and proposes himself to me. The fact that this proposal is
constantly repeated to me constantly invites me, at
the very least, to the duty of inquiry. There is no
escaping from this proposal. We must choose either
adherence, which establishes its own precise drama,
the drama of commitment and holiness, or *quest*,
which is just as laden with consequences. For the
very fact that we are born into a Christian climate,
into a Christian tradition, means that there is not one

single thing that we may address independently from it. It is, therefore, necessary to constantly apply oneself to this proposal, with an engagement that is, for one thing, a necessary condition for taking part in bringing about a society.

The features of engagement with a proposal like this come from what the proposal itself requires. It is not up to us to define what we must do to feel right in our minds. We cannot be the ones to determine, by the work of our own imaginations, the ways of carrying out the verification we have to do. Rather, the contours of the proposal itself establish the method we must follow.

In actuality, the Christian proposal corresponds to a human reality present in the world around us. This proposal has a face, and when we fail to consider it, we betray the proposal. This face is the community of the Church. Only by applying ourselves and our lives totally to the community of the Church — to this mystery of God in the world, to this constant, unswerving emergence of the proposal of Christ through the centuries — can we carry out a serious comparison and generate an adequate evaluation of the tradition into which we come to be.

The face of this proposal changes, but nevertheless it remains one: the one mystery of the Church, a visible, tactile Reality. This reality needs to be lived. It demands that we engage it, applying our whole selves. In other words, we have to enter into it and compare all its manifestations, all its suggestions, and all its directives with the ultimate needs of our own humanity. And to the extent we discover that these suggestions, these instructions, and these initiatives answer our authentic human needs (and, therefore, enhance them), adherence and conviction will open up within us, and grow increasingly serious and conclusive. So, this is not a matter of studying theology or forming an association. It is everything. It takes all of life to make the proposal truly reach us, and to make it come to us as new life, as the birth of a new human being. To be "convinced" means that all one's self is "bound," connected, to something. Thus we will be entirely bound to this Reality. The Reality becomes us, until we will feel that we are that Reality.

Of course, the mystery of God's will could allow this "crisis," this engaged "sifting," to end in a separation, to end with an opposing and painful choice. But in these cases there is a symptom that reveals that someone is choosing separation with faithfulness; that is, after having sincerely engaged with the worldview into which they were born. That symptom is sorrow about the separation and a deeper friendship with their origins. And there is an experience that, even in its generality, sums up all of what people discover through "critical" engagement with the Christian tradition they inherited – that is, the awareness of being appreciated as a person, as a singularity and at the same time as solidarity with the cosmos, loving participation in the cosmos. It is recognition of their personal authenticity and their role in the world.

This brings to mind the words of Jesus: "Whoever follows me will have eternal life and one hundred times more now in this present age."[2] We might almost be tempted to object, like Nicodemus: "How can this happen?"[3] The answer remains the same: "Come and see." That is, "Follow me and you will see." It calls for a willingness to apply ourselves that, much as it involves a working relationship, as we might call it, nonetheless implies throwing our entire life into the community of the Church, and seeing the life of the Church community as our own life. Then we "see"; that is, then we understand what the Church is for us.

It is a true "verification" to carry out.

Applying ourselves as a tool for verification

In short, everything has to be consciously framed as "verification," as a test of the value of the Christian tradition. Today nothing is more important than applying ourselves as living parts of the Church community. But the great community of the Church would be a distant and abstract thing if it did not emerge right here, where we are. For this reason, nothing is more important than helping to render the Church community present, or to bring it to life in our environment, through the "crisis" of our engagement with it.

Those who do not go through this process of applying themselves will either stay Christian without ever saying anything new, or leave.

The only way to avoid being "alienated" in this society, with its terrible instruments of invasion, is to have a sense for the meaning of history, to live our own "crisis" in a genuine way, by applying ourselves adequately to the tradition into which we are born, to the Christian proposal. And it is magnificent that this proposal, in particular, unlike all others, is so concrete in nature, so existential. It is magnificent that it is a community in the world, a world within the world, a different reality within reality. And not different because it has different interests, but different because it has a different way of fulfilling the interests it shares with everyone else.

II. Dialogical Openness

An idea of dialogue

If we were entirely cut off from the world and other people, and human beings were alone, absolutely alone, we would never discover anything new. Newness always comes from an encounter with another. This is the rule that life is born with: we exist because other people have given us life. An isolated seed will not grow. If, however, it is placed in the conditions to be prompted by something else, then it sprouts. The figure of the other is crucial in order for my life to develop, in order for what I am to become dynamism and life. This relationship with the "other," whoever they may be, is *dialogue*.

What does the other bring to the dialogue? Certainly they always bring a certain set of interests that is, as such, partial. But within the entire network of ordered relationships, they help to co-create a holistic maturity, a wholeness. Each one of us, precisely because we are individuals, each with a set disposition, tends to place emphasis on certain things. Contact with others calls our attention to other things, or to other facets of the same things, making dialogue a function of the parameters of universality and totality, for which human beings are destined. And let us not forget how important a role dialogue plays for the catholicity of the Church.

The condition for dialogue

Unlimited openness, which is proper to dialogue as both a developmental element of the human person and an element that creates a new society, has a crucial requirement: self-awareness. True dialogue can only exist to the extent that I bring *an awareness of myself*. That is, something is dialogue if it is carried out as a comparison between the other's proposal and an awareness of the proposal represented by me – the proposal that I am. That is, something can only be dialogue to the extent that I am mature in my self-awareness. For this reason, if a "crisis" (in the sense of applying myself to sifting my own tradition) does not logically precede my dialogue with someone else, one of two things will happen. Either I will be ensnared by the other's influence, or, in my rejection of the other, I will fall into an irrationally rigid defence of my position. Therefore, it is true that dialogue always entails openness toward the other, whoever they may be, because everyone else testifies to an interest or an aspect that we would have left out. Therefore, everyone provokes us toward a more complete overall comparison. But dialogue also requires my own maturity, a critical awareness of what I am.

If we fail to keep this in mind, we face an extremely grave danger: that of *confusing dialogue with compromise*. Indeed, using what we have in common with another person as a starting point does not necessarily mean saying the same thing, even if we are using the same words. The justice of others is not Christian justice. The freedom of others is not Christian freedom. Education as understood by others is not education as understood by the Church.

There is, to borrow a term from scholastic philosophy, a different *form* in the words that we use. That is, there is a different form in our way of perceiving, sensing, and facing the world.

We should not so much look for what we have in common with others in their ideology, but in their native structure – in their human needs, the original criteria that make them human beings like us. Openness in dialogue, therefore, means knowing to start from the solutions proposed, either by the other's ideology or by our Christianity. This is because truly diverse conceptions of the world have nothing in common, except the humanity of the people who cling to them as vessels of hope or of answers.

This last point is an important one, because the concepts of democracy and openness, as they are understood by a widespread mentality among us, tend to diminish the concept of dialogue. The people we tend to think of as "democratic" are relativists, regardless of their particular version of relativism. Conversely, we tend to consider anyone who asserts an absolute to be antidemocratic (intolerant and dogmatic).

Some years ago, a famous professor, addressing a highly educated audience in Milan, went so far as to say: "Catholics, for the very fact that they are Catholic, cannot be citizens of a democratic state. Catholics claim to know the truth, the absolute. It is, therefore, impossible to have a dialogue with them, and, therefore, also impossible to co-exist democratically with them."

This mentality, or compromising with it, gives rise to the attempt to characterize as "open-minded" anyone who is inclined to "set aside anything not agreed upon, and to consider only those things upon which people agree," and anyone inclined to set aside the vision of life they have. This attempt is full of misunderstandings.

In our Christian mentality, democracy is living together; that is, recognizing that my life implies the existence of others. And the tool of this living together is dialogue. Now, dialogue is my proposal of what I see to another, and my care for what others experience because of my respect for their humanity and a love I bear them that does not at all entail a doubt about me, that does not at all entail compromising what I am.

This is the openness created by the Christian mindset. It starts by affirming the unity of human nature – in its origin, values, and destiny – beyond any ideology, and it proclaims, as the law of relationships, the affirmation of the person, and, therefore, the affirmation, above all, of people's freedom.

Democracy cannot be founded interiorly upon a set number of ideological ideas held in common. What it can be founded on is charity; that is, the love of human beings, the rationally sufficient basis of which is the human relationship with God.

III. Conclusion

Under this view, therefore, two basic elements are necessary in order to build a new society. First, to live Christian community in the environment. That is, to finally discover that "crisis" or "critique" concerning one's own Christianity means understanding Christianity as a proposal to all of one's life (to live every interest according to the suggestion of the Christian communities). Thus, it is a proposal to apply all one's life to it, at least as a working hypothesis.

We must carry out this work with care and total openness, with a freedom of spirit that allows us to express our Christianity in a living way and to translate it into forms that may be new. This means immediately abandoning old forms, if the circumstances require it, with the readiness and agility Jesus mentions in the Gospel when he says that Christianity and the life he has brought are like an ever-new wine, and that no one pours new wine into old wineskins, nor do they use new cloth to patch old cloth, since *peior scissura fit*[4]; that is, doing so would only make matters worse.

Chapter Three

The Structure of Experience

Experience as the development of the person

Before, the person did not exist. Therefore, what makes up the person is a *given*, the product of an *other*.

This original situation is repeated at every stage of human development. What provokes my growth is not me; it is other than me.

In the concrete, experience means living what makes me grow.

Thus, experience brings about the growth of the person through the appreciation of an objective relationship.

Note well: "experience" thus entails the fact of *realizing that we are growing*. And realizing it in its two basic aspects: the ability to understand and the ability to love.

a) The person is, above all, awareness. Because of this, what characterizes experience is not so much doing, is not so much establishing relationships with reality, as a mechanical fact. This is the error inherent in the typical expression "to have an experience," where "experience" equates to trying things out.

Rather, what characterizes experience is *understanding* something, discovering its *meaning*. Thus, experience entails an intelligence concerning the meaning of things. And something's meaning is discovered in its connection with all the rest. Thus, experience means discovering the purpose of a particular thing in the context of the world.

b) It is not we who create something's meaning. Its connection with all other things takes the form of an objective bond. Thus, true experience entails saying yes to a situation that beckons. Experience means taking what is said to us and making it our own. Therefore, while it does mean making things ours, it also means doing so in such a way as to walk within their objective meaning, and this meaning is the Word of an Other.

True experience mobilizes and increases our capacity to adhere, our capacity to love.

True experience plunges into the rhythm of reality, and makes us strain irresistibly toward unification up to the ultimate aspect of things; that is, up to the true and complete meaning of a thing.

Nature as the locus of experience

"Nature" is what we call the locus (or place) of the objective relationships that cause the person to develop. That is, "nature" is the locus of experience.

The characteristic of nature is that it builds an organic and hierarchical fabric that stimulates the need for immanent unity in every person.

This existential need corresponds to the affirmation of God. God is precisely the holistic meaning to which nature, in its objective organicness, beckons the human mind.

Error in human experience

The need for unity – the driver of the thinking life of a person – must struggle against the forces of division that are also present in the human being. These forces push us to disregard objective connections and to destroy the organicness of the fabric of nature, isolating its individual elements.

Because of the human need for unity mentioned above, when a single relationship is taken in isolation, we inevitably tend to make it absolute.

This blocks the dynamism of the person's evolutionary relationships, turning it into a series of disjoined partialities, with exaggerated affirmations of this or that.

This leads to many inadequate, if common, usages of the word "experience." These include using it to mean an immediate reaction to a certain proposal, or the proliferation of connections that occurs as the simple outcome of multiplying initiatives, or the spontaneous attraction or disgust one feels for something new, or the affirmation of one's own explanation or framework, or a memory of the past that is not relived as a present value, or even an event that is referred to in order to block a particular aspiration or to undermine ideals.

The mystery of God revealed in human experience

The intervention of the prophets and of Christ in history had the function of pointing to God, with absolute clarity, as the ultimate implication of human experience, and, therefore, to religiosity as an inevitable dimension of authentic, holistic experience.

But when it comes to Christ, his exceptionality lies not so much in the fact that he serves as a reminder of that implication, but rather in the fact that his occurrence is the physical presence of that ultimate meaning of history.

There is no totally complete human experience that is not an appreciation – whether conscious or unconscious – of the relationship with this fact that is the man-Christ.

Nature is no longer the only locus of the objective relationship that causes the human person to grow. There is also a "supernatural" locus. The history of this locus is called Church (the "mystical body of Christ").

Christian experience

The experience of Christianity and the Church occurs as a single, vital act, and it is composed of three elements:

a) An *encounter* with an objective fact originally independent from the person having the experience. The existential reality of this fact is a tangible community, as with every wholly human reality. The human voice of authority in the judgments and directives of this community constitute its criterion and form.

There is no version of Christian experience, no matter how interior, that does not entail, at least in the ultimate sense, the encounter with the community and the reference to authority.

b) The power to adequately perceive the meaning of this encounter. We cannot sufficiently understand the value of the fact we come across in an encounter without a gesture of God. Indeed, the same gesture with which God makes himself present to humanity in the Christian event also enhances the mind's cognitive capacities, tuning the penetration of the human gaze upon the exceptional reality that has provoked it. We call this *the grace of faith*.

c) *Awareness of the correspondence* between the meaning of the Fact we have come across and the meaning of our own existence, between the Christian and ecclesial reality and our own person, between the Encounter and our own destiny.

It is our awareness of this correspondence that verifies the growth of self that is essential to the phenomenon of experience.

In Christian experience – more than any other – we clearly see how human self-awareness and critical thinking are engaged in an authentic experience. We also see how very different an authentic experience is from identifying ourselves with an impression we have had or from reducing ourselves to an emotional reaction.

It is through this "verification" that, in Christian experience, the mystery of divine initiative essentially valorizes human reason.

And it is in this "verification" that human *freedom* shows itself: because we may only notice and recognize the enhancing correspondence between the present mystery and our own human dynamism to the extent that we nurture a present and alive acceptance of our basic dependency, our essential "having been made." Simplicity and "purity of heart" – "poverty of spirit" – consist in this acceptance.

All the drama of freedom lies in this "poverty of spirit," and it is a drama so profound that it plays out almost furtively.

Luigi Giussani

A Brief Biography

1922   15 October: Luigi Giussani is born in Desio (Milan) to Angelina Gelosa and Beniamino Giussani. At Giussani's funeral on 24 February 2005, then-Cardinal Joseph Ratzinger (who would become Pope Benedict XVI) gave a homily in which he talked about the family environment that Giussani was raised in: "Father Giussani grew up in a house that was – to use his words – poor in bread but rich in music, so that from the very beginning he was touched, or, better, wounded, by the desire for beauty."

      19 October: Baptism in the parish church of Saints Siro and Materno in Desio.

1933   2 October: Enters the diocesan seminary of San Pietro Martire (Saint Peter Martyr) in Seveso, where he attends the first four years of *ginnasio* (sixth through ninth grades, 1933–37).

1937   Transfers to the seminary in Venegono, where he will spend eight years: the last year of *ginnasio*, three of high school (1938–41), and six of advanced theological study (1941–47). Fr. Giussani would later recall that, in him, "everything is due to the faithfulness of certain teaching, the teaching I received in my years of high school and diocesan seminary in Venegono, from true teachers who knew how to help me internalize a solid Christian tradition."

1939   Founds the group Studium Christi, together with some friends, and the newsletter *Christus*. "One winter evening in seminary, after dinner (we had about an hour of free time then), Enrico Manfredini and another classmate, De Ponti, came up to me and said: 'Listen, if Christ is everything, what does he have to do with mathematics?' We were not yet sixteen. Everything in my life came about from that question."

1943   Receives the equivalent of a bachelor's degree.

1944   Starts the group S. Giosafat pro Unità delle Chiese (Saint Josaphat for the Unity of Churches).

1945   26 May: Is ordained a priest by Cardinal Ildefonso Schuster, in the Duomo of Milan. Receives his teaching license in theology and begins teaching in the minor seminary of Seveso. His studies focus on Eastern theology (particularly Slavic), American Protestant theology, and the analysis of the rational motives for adhering to faith and the Church. Begins serving in a parish on the outskirts of Milan on Saturdays and Sundays, but is soon forced to leave this work because of the onset of serious pulmonary issues.

1946   Begins a series of long periods of illness, spent mostly in Varigotti, on the Italian Riviera, which last until 1949.

1950   Having regained his health, he begins teaching in the seminary again. In the confessional he meets his first high school students, who live in the Milan parish where he serves as a pastoral assistant on Saturdays and Sundays.

1951   The first of his series of studies on Protestantism and Orthodoxy are published.

While travelling by train toward Rimini, he meets a group of high school students and starts conversing with them about Christianity: "I was instantly surprised by their vast, cosmic, and frightening ignorance." After this chance encounter on the train, he develops the desire to dedicate himself to the education of young people.

1953   Is invited to take part in the Council of Student Youth (Gioventù Studentesca, or GS), which brings together high school students in Catholic Action (Azione Cattolica) in Milan.

1954   Receives his doctorate in theology with the highest possible grade (70/70), magna cum laude, after defending a dissertation on "The Christian meaning of man according to Reinhold Niebuhr."

In the years that follow, Giussani will continue to study American Protestantism, a sign of the ecumenism that he always understood as "passion for unity." His writings and research on Orthodoxy can be understood in the same vein.

Begins teaching religion at the Berchet classical high school in Milan. "I remember it as if it were today: Berchet Classical High School, 9 a.m., the first day of school, October 1954. I remember the feeling I had as I climbed the few steps up to the door to the school: it was the naïveté of a certain enthusiasm, of a brashness, which had made me leave behind the path of teaching theology in the diocesan seminary of Venegono, although I loved it, in order to help young people to rediscover the terms of a real faith, with my heart bursting from the thought that Christ is everything for human lives; Christ is the heart of human life." For him, this news had to reach those kids, for their happiness.

Over the years he will go on to teach at other Milan schools as well. The contents of his classes are the topics that will accompany him throughout all of his human trajectory, as a priest and educator: the religious sense and the reasonableness of faith, the hypothesis and the reality of Revelation, the teaching of Christ in revealing himself, and the Church's nature as the continuation of Christ's presence in history until the present day. Above all he as a person exerts an attraction that makes the Christian announcement contemporary to the young people who meet him. Early on they number only a few dozen, but over the years they will become hundreds and, later, thousands of people fascinated by his proposal of a living Christianity and by his method: faith as experience, the announcement of Jesus Christ, centre of the cosmos and of history, and Christianity presented not first as doctrine and a set of moral rules, but as the occurrence of an encounter, perfectly in tune with the later teachings of Popes John Paul II, Benedict XVI, and Francis.

1955   Is named Diocesan Assistant to Student Youth (GS). Publishes *Risposte cristiane ai problemi dei giovani* (Christian answers to the problems of young people).

1956   Moves out of the seminary and takes up residence in Milan.

1957   Leaves his teaching position in Venegono.

As head of GS, he renews its educational proposal. He involves GS students in an educational gesture involving charity, dubbed Caritativa, or "Charitable Work" in English, in the depressed area on Milan's outskirts known as the "Bassa."

Publishes *The Religious Sense*, drawing on his experience during his first years of teaching. Later editions of the work will go into greater depth to expand on the contents and concerns of that first version.

1958   A small group forms around Giussani who will become the first members of the Adult Group, or Memores Domini (people who live out total dedication to Christ and the Church in virginity, following the teachings of the Gospels, living in the world like any other laypeople).

1959   Publishes the first of three short books that summarize the core of his proposal, and which will go on to be central texts throughout the history of the as-yet-unfounded Comunione e Liberazione (Communion and Liberation) Movement: *G.S. Riflessioni sopra un'esperienza* (G.S. Reflections on an experience), 1959; *Tracce d'esperienza cristiana* (Traces of Christian experience), 1960; and *Appunti di metodo cristiano* (Notes on Christian method), 1964. All are published with the imprimatur of the Church.

1960   First trip to Brazil, in anticipation of the departure of the first young people from GS, invited by Monsignor Aristide Pirovano, Bishop of Macapá.

1962   When the Second Vatican Council begins in 1962, Giussani and GS are watching and ready to receive its basic concerns and pastoral instructions. "From the Council, we wished to embrace its central instruction through and through: to reclaim an awareness of the mission of the Church, addressed to each person and to all people."

1964   The Adult Group is born.
Begins teaching Introduction to Theology at the Catholic University of the Sacred Heart of Milan. Becomes involved with the group of young college graduates who have started the Charles Péguy Cultural Centre.

1965   Spends the summer in the United States in order to

learn American forms of parish associations and to expand his study of American Protestantism, for the purpose of completing a new research work, necessary for obtaining a position as lecturer.

On his return to Italy, he leaves his leadership role in GS. The organization is showing symptoms of strife, which will come to a head in the crisis of 1968.

1967   Stops teaching at Berchet high school.

1968   As student protests drag on for many months, and many young people abandon GS, Giussani lays the foundations for a recovery of the original experience of the Movement. "Christianity is that 'what' which makes tradition into a living reality, which turns the articulation of thought into a living reality, which brings to life what is past. It's what makes thought, idea and value come alive. But alive means present! We can employ no other means – if we do not want to flounder in confusion – than to return to our origins: how did Christianity arise, how did it begin? It was an event. Christianity is an event."

1969   The name Comunione e Liberazione (CL) is used for the Movement for the first time in a flyer written by students at the State University of Milan who have kept up ties with Fr. Giussani and who perceive and take up the initial idea that had given rise to GS. From now on it will be the name of the movement led by Fr. Giussani.

Publishes *American Protestant Theology: A Historical Sketch*. To this day the book is one of the most thorough works on the topic published in Italy.

Publishes *Reinhold Niebuhr*.

1971   Plays a role in the foundation of the Cascinazza Benedictine monastery outside Milan.

Meets the Archbishop of Krakow, Karol Wojtyla (who

will become Pope John Paul II), in Poland.

Meets the Swiss theologian Hans Urs von Balthasar, who introduces him to Joseph Ratzinger (who will become Pope Benedict XVI).

1975   Forms a friendship with some Spanish families who will form the first group of CL in Spain.

23 March: Travels in pilgrimage, together with the entire Movement, to Saint Peter's Square in Rome, at the behest of Pope Paul VI, who exchanges words with Giussani at the end of the event, encouraging him to proceed along the path he began with GS and then with CL: "Take heart, you and your young people, because this is the right road." That day Fr. Giussani said: "Little by little, as we mature we become a spectacle to ourselves and, God willing, we become a spectacle to others, too. A spectacle of limitation, of betrayal, and because of this of an affable and impassioned humiliation. And, at the same time, a spectacle of inexhaustible certainty in that Grace that is given to us and renewed in the awareness of each morning. This is where our characteristic, naïve self-confidence comes from, thanks to which every day of our life is thought of and desired, despite everything, as an offering to God so that the Church may exist, within our bodies, within our souls, through the materialness of our existence."

1976   Speaks at the assembly of leaders of the university students of CL, in a major turning point for the history of the Movement. "Our identity is identifying with Christ. Identifying with Christ is the constitutive dimension of our person. If Christ defines my personality, you, who are seized by him, must necessarily enter into the dimension of my personality. This is the 'new creature' of the wonderful last part of the letter to the Galatians, the beginning of the 'new creation' St. James talks about. 'The victory that conquers the world is our faith,' says John."

1977   Publishes *The Risk of Education*, culling his reflections from his more than twenty years of experience as an educator, first at the high school level and then at the university. It will be one of his most widely read books: "The primary concern of a true and sufficient education is that of *educating the human heart as God made it*. Since my first hour in the classroom I have always said: 'I am not here to make you adopt the ideas I will give you as your own, but to teach you a true method for judging the things I will say. And the things that I will say are an experience, which is the outcome of a long past: two thousand years.' Respect for this method has defined our commitment to education since the beginning, clearly indicating its purpose: to demonstrate how faith is relevant to life's needs. Because of my formation at home and in seminary, first, and my own reflections later, I was deeply convinced that, unless faith could be found and located in present experience, and confirmed by it, and be useful for responding to its needs, it would not be able to endure in a world where everything, *everything*, said and says the opposite."

1979   18 January: Private audience with Pope John Paul II. "As soon as I left the audience, in the heart of my joy I felt a sense of great responsibility: a desire to serve that man with all my strength and with all my life. My friends, let us serve this man, let us serve Christ in this great man with our whole existence."

31 March: Accompanies the CL university students to their first audience with Pope John Paul II. In the upcoming years he will often visit the Pope with groups of young people.

The bishop of Piacenza, Monsignor Enrico Manfredini, recognizes the Memores Domini consecrated lay adult group.

Organizes the first international conference of movements in Rome, together with the Polish priest Fr. Blachnicki, founder of the Light-Life Movement.

1982   11 February: Encouraged by John Paul II, the Pontifical Council for the Laity officially recognizes the Fraternity of Communion and Liberation, with Giussani as founder and president for life. "What happened on February 11 is surely the greatest grace in the entire history of the Movement. The certainty in the value of our experience implied by this event pushes us with greater peace and generosity of heart to that obedience to the bishops and cooperation with their guidance without which the building of God's people becomes uncertain."

1983   Pope John Paul II makes him a Monsignor, with the title of Honorary Prelate of His Holiness.

1984   Speaks at the Youth Day Jubilee as part of the Holy Year of Redemption.

Leads CL in a pilgrimage to Rome for an audience with Pope John Paul II for the thirtieth anniversary of the Movement. The Pope says: "'Go out to all nations,' Christ told his disciples (Mt 28:19). And I repeat to you: 'Go out to all the world and bring the truth, the beauty, and the peace that meet in Christ redeemer.' This is the charge I leave you today." Fr. Giussani embraces this task, and, for CL, this is the beginning of a season of missionary activity that will bring its members to countries throughout the world.

1985   Is named a Consultor of the Pontifical Council for the Laity.

Attends a meeting of the Nueva Tierra cultural association in Avila, Spain, among the leaders of which is Fr. Julián Carrón. Giussani affirms: "We are what you are: our story and yours have the same roots, the same principles, and the very same end. Because what is needed the most in the Church today is this: that a great movement of friends spring up [...] in which faith goes back to being what it was in the first centuries: the discovery of a more human humanity." In September, Nueva Tierra will join CL.

1986   A new edition of *The Religious Sense* is published.
Goes on pilgrimage to the Holy Land together with a group of adults in CL.

1987   Travels to Japan at the invitation of the mayor of Nagoya. Meets one of the leaders of Japanese Buddhism, Shōdō Habukawa.
Attends the Bishops Synod on the Laity as a member nominated by the pontiff. "What is Christianity if not the event of a new person who, by nature, becomes a new protagonist on the world scene? The preeminent issue of the whole Christian matter is the occurrence of the new creature that St. Paul talks about, for laypersons, too. What is missing is not so much the verbal or cultural repetition of the announcement. People today are waiting, perhaps unconsciously, for the experience of encounter with people for whom the fact of Christ is a reality so present that their life is changed. Human impact is what can jolt people today – an event that reechoes an initial event, when Jesus raised his eyes and said: 'Zacchaeus, come down here, I'm coming to your house.'"

1988   The Memores Domini group is approved by the Holy See as a private universal ecclesial association, with Giussani as its founder and president for life.
Publishes *At the Origin of the Christian Claim*.

1990   Publishes *Why the Church?*

1991   Undergoes surgery to remove a tumour. Begins to show
        early signs of Parkinson's Disease.

        Stops teaching at the Catholic University, having
        reached the mandatory retirement age.

1992   Leads a pilgrimage to Lourdes to celebrate ten years of
        the CL Fraternity. This is the supreme Christian task:
        "Not that of being a mother or a father, not that of being
        a journalist or an engineer, not that of being a soldier or
        a laborer, not that of being the winner of elections or the
        slave of masters. None of these. Our task is to spread the
        great message of Christ in the world."

1993   The Holy See recognizes the institute of the Sisters of
        Charity of the Assumption, which Giussani has had ties
        with since 1958.

        The book series titled Books of the Christian Spirit,
        directed by Giussani and published by Rizzoli publish-
        ing house, publishes the first of what will eventually
        number more than eighty volumes.

1994   Is named a consultor of the Congregation for the
        Clergy.

        Publishes *Is It Possible to Live This Way? An Unusual
        Approach to Christian Existence*. It is about a path toward
        the theological virtues, developed over the course of a
        year in the relationship between Giussani and about one
        hundred young people who had decided to give their
        lives to Christ in a form of total dedication, in virginity.

1995   Invites the leaders of CL in Spain to take part in the
        leadership of the Movement's International Committee.

        Begins publishing frequent articles in secular newspapers
        il Giornale, la Repubblica, and the *Corriere della Sera*.

1996   Undergoes extensive testing to identify the cause of his
        worsening health.

1997   The musical series Spirto Gentil is launched in CD form with the release of Pergolesi's *Stabat Mater*, edited by Giussani with Deutsche Grammophon and some other record labels. The series will go on to release fifty-two CDs.

The English edition of *The Religious Sense* is presented at the UN headquarters in New York.

1998   30 May: Addresses the gathering of ecclesial movements and new communities with Pope John Paul II in St. Peter's Square, contributing his testimony: "It was a simplicity of heart that made me feel and recognize Christ as exceptional. Because that Man, Jesus of Nazareth, is the Reality on which all the positivity of every man's existence depends. The Mystery as mercy remains the last word even on all the awful possibilities of history. For this reason existence expresses itself, as ultimate ideal, in *begging*. The real protagonist of history is the beggar: Christ who begs for man's heart, and man's heart that begs for Christ."

Undergoes surgery to remove a tumour.

1999   The English edition of *At the Origin of the Christian Claim* is presented in New York at the UN.

2001   11 September: After the terrorist attack on the United States that destroyed lower Manhattan, he dictates a message for all the North American CL communities. "This moment is at least as serious as the destruction of Jerusalem. It is entirely within God's Mystery. God's mercy is the greatest word."

2002   11 February: Pope John Paul II sends him a long personal letter on the occasion of the twentieth anniversary of pontifical recognition of the CL Fraternity. "As I go back in memory over the life and works of the Fraternity and the Movement, the first aspect that strikes me is the commitment you have put into listening to the needs of today's man. Man never stops seeking: both when he is marked by the drama of violence, loneliness and insignificance, and when he lives in serenity and joy, he continues to seek. The only answer which can satisfy him and appease this search of his comes from the encounter with the One who is at the source of his being and his action. The Movement, therefore, has chosen and chooses to indicate not a road, but the road towards a solution to this existential drama. The road, as you have affirmed so many times, is Christ."

15 October: Receives a personal letter from Pope John Paul II and thousands of notes from around the world for his eightieth birthday. That day he said of himself, to the daily newspaper *Avvenire*: "Everything happened for me in the most absolute normality, and the things that happened astonished me while they were happening because it was so clear that it was God who was doing them, turning them into the fabric of a story that happened to me – that happens to me – right before my eyes."

2003   Writes a reflection on the funeral of Italian military personnel killed in the assault on Nasiriyah, Iraq, for Channel 2 news: "How terrible! How shameful! If there were an education of the people, everyone would be better off."

2004   Writes his last letter to Pope John Paul II, on the occasion of the fiftieth anniversary of the birth of the Movement. "Not only did I have no intention of 'founding' anything, but I believe that the genius of the Movement that I saw coming to birth lies in having felt the urgency to proclaim the need to return to the elementary aspects of Christianity, that is to say, the passion of the Christian fact as such in its original elements, and nothing more."

Obtains permission from the Archbishop of Madrid for Fr. Julián Carrón to move to Milan to help him oversee the entire Movement.

Writes his last letter to the entire Movement on the occasion of the CL pilgrimage to Loreto for the fiftieth anniversary of the Fraternity.

24 December: writes a reflection for the Channel 2 Christmas program. "Christmas is Christ's love for humanity. A new Being comes into the world, the world of the true God."

In late December his health rapidly deteriorates.

2005   18 February: After receiving news of Giussani's decline, Pope John Paul II sends him a telegram invoking the protection of the Virgin Mary *Salus infirmorum* (health of the sick).

22 February: Dies at his home in Milan.

24 February: Funeral in the Duomo of Milan celebrated by then-Cardinal-Prefect of the Congregation for the Doctrine of the Faith Joseph Ratzinger, who delivered the eulogy, acting as personal emissary of Pope John Paul II. "By guiding people not to himself but to Christ he has truly conquered hearts, he has helped to make the world better, he has helped to open up the doors of the world to heaven."

Remembering Fr. Giussani at the end of the funeral, Fr. Carrón says: "We shall never be able to forget the fever of life we have experienced beside you. In contact with his experience of faith, we saw happening in us, to our astonishment, something we could not imagine, but secretly desired. The same human vibration that runs through the Gospels we detected in ourselves as well. This is how he taught us to know and love Jesus. Christ became more fascinating for us every time, the dearest Presence."

Buried in the Famedio monument in the Monumental Cemetery of Milan, in the space reserved for illustrious citizens of the city.

2008   Giussani's casket is transferred to a newly built chapel within the Monumental Cemetery. From the day of his burial, his grave becomes a site of constant pilgrimage from people in Italy and all over the world.

2012   22 February: At the end of a Mass in the Duomo of Milan held to celebrate the seventh anniversary of Fr. Giussani's death, Fr. Julián Carrón, president of the CL Fraternity, announces that he has submitted a request to open the cause for beatification and canonization of Fr. Giussani. The request was accepted by the archbishop of Milan, Cardinal Angelo Scola.
Father Giussani is "Servant of God."

Further information may be found in Alberto Savorana's book *The Life of Luigi Giussani*. Montreal: McGill–Queen's University Press 2017.

For the complete bibliography of Luigi Giussani and the editorial history of his works, see the following website: www.scritti.luigigiussani.org

Works of Fr. Giussani available in English:

The Religious Sense. Montreal: McGill–Queen's University Press 1997

At the Origin of the Christian Claim. Montreal: McGill–Queen's University Press 1998

Why the Church? Montreal: McGill–Queen's University Press 2001

The Journey to Truth is an Experience. Montreal: McGill–Queen's University Press 2006

Is It Possible to Live This Way? Volume 1: Faith. Montreal: McGill–Queen's University Press 2008

Is It Possible to Live This Way? Volume 2: Hope. Montreal: McGill–Queen's University Press 2008

Is It Possible to Live This Way? Volume 3: Charity. Montreal: McGill–Queen's University Press 2009

American Protestant Theology. Montreal: McGill–Queen's University Press 2014

Christ, God's Companionship with Man. Montreal: McGill–Queen's University Press 2015

Generating Traces in the History of the World (with Stefano Alberto and Javier Prades). Montreal: McGill–Queen's University Press 2010

Notes

Foreword

1 Over the years I have written a series of essays about the church and the kind of education we find in modern universities. See, for example, my "How Christian Universities Contribute to the Corruption of the Youth," *Christian Existence Today: Essays on Church, World, and Living in Between* (Grand Rapids: Brazos Press, 2001), 237–53; "The Politics of Witness: How We Educate Christians in Liberal Societies," in *After Christendom?* (Nashville: Abingdon, 1999), 133–54; "Christians in the Hands of Flaccid Secularists: Theology and 'Moral Inquiry' in the Modern University" and "Christian Schooling, or Making Students Dysfunctional," in *Sanctify Them in the Truth: Holiness Exemplified* (Nashville: Abingdon, 1998), 201–26.

2 I am, of course, aware that the focus of Giussani's work is on the education of students at younger ages than college students. However, I think it is not unreasonable for me to focus on "higher education," not only because I know it best, but more importantly because what happens in universities usually has a direct effect on secondary education.

Teachers in secondary education too often reproduce the mistakes they learned at the university. So the miseducation begun in college is passed on to students in lower grades, which means they will have no resources to challenge the education they later receive in college.

3 Robert Wuthnow, *The Restructuring of American Religion* (Princeton: Princeton University Press, 1988), 160.

4 Even if the college-educated continue to identify with a church, Wuthnow's study clearly indicates that they are less likely to identify with Christian orthodoxy.

5 Douglas Sloan, *Faith and Knowledge: Mainline Protestantism and Higher Education* (Louisville: Westminster/John Knox Press, 1994).

6 Alasdair MacIntyre, "Catholic Universities: Dangers, Hopes, Choices," in *Higher Learning and Catholic Traditions*, ed. Robert E. Sullivan (Notre Dame: University of Notre Dame Press, 2001), 5–6. MacIntyre provides a useful tool to test how far a university has moved to this fragmented condition. He asks whether a wonderful and effective undergraduate teacher who can communicate how his or her discipline contributes to an integrated account of things – but whose publishing consists of one original but brilliant article on how to teach – would receive tenure. Or would tenure be granted to a professor who is unable or unwilling to teach undergraduates, preferring to teach only advanced graduate students and engaged in "cutting-edge research." MacIntyre suggests if the answers to these two inquiries are "No" and "Yes," you can be sure you are at a university, at least if it is a Catholic university, in need of serious reform (p. 6). I feel quite confident that MacIntyre learned to put the matter this way by serving on the Faculty Appointments, Promotion, and Tenure Committee of Duke University. I am confident that this is the source of his understanding of the increasing subdisciplinary character of fields,

because I also served on that committee for seven years. During that time I observed people becoming "leaders" in their fields by making their work so narrow that the "field" consisted of no more than five or six people. We would often hear from the chairs of the departments that they could not understand what the person was doing, but they were sure the person to be considered for tenure was the best "in his or her field."

7 MacIntyre, "Catholic Universities," 5.

8 MacIntyre, "Catholic Universities," 4.

9 I will make my references to Giussani in internal footnotes in the text.

10 Though I think MacIntyre would largely agree with Giussani's position, I am not sure he would be willing to say as Giussani does that faith is the highest form of rationality. MacIntyre argues that philosophy is a strictly secular discipline, which means his arguments concerning how philosophy is properly understood do not draw on any theological presuppositions. According to MacIntyre, "this is a universe that is at once Catholic and secular, in which purpose is at home, in which human and other goods are integral to the intelligible order of things, and in which the project of making that order of things intelligible to us through the activities of enquiry proper to universities is itself to be understood as a part of the order of things" (p. 4). I have no doubt that MacIntyre would not think this means that faith is irrational, but I am not sure if MacIntyre would think that faith is as rational as the "secular" discipline of philosophy. One catches a hint in MacIntyre from time to time that he may have a far too strict distinction between nature and grace.

11 Giussani made the comments in a talk to teachers in 1977. This text was published as an appendix in the 1995 edition of *The Risk of Education*. See L. Giussani, *Il rischio educativo: Come creazione di personalità e storia* (Turin: SEI, 1995), 85.

12 Giussani, *Il rischio educativo*, 86.

13 See, for example, my *With the Grain of the Universe: The Church's Witness and Natural Theology* (Grand Rapids: Brazos Press, 2001).

14 Giussani, *Il rischio educativo*, 85.

15 MacIntyre, "Catholic Universities," 8.

16 Giussani defines culture "as the critical, systematic development of an experience. An experience is an event that opens us up to the totality of reality: experience always implies a comparison between what one feels and what one believes to be the ultimate ideal or meaning. Culture works to unfold this implication for wholeness and totality which is part of every human experience" (*Il rischio educativo*, p. 135). I am much more hesitant than Giussani to make culture depend on "experience" because, particularly in liberal Protestantism, "experience" replaces the church as the ultimate appeal.

17 The presence of Christians in an intellectual endeavour no longer insures such work can be trusted to represent the "following" Giussani rightly thinks characteristic of Christian convictions. Moreover, work done by non-Christians may well reflect a more determined Christian perspective than that done by Christians, which is but a reminder that these are complex matters.

18 Indeed the very language of values – that is, the assumption that the moral life consists in subjective desires – is an indication that the language of economics has subverted serious moral judgments.

19 Alasdair MacIntyre wonderfully develops the interrelation of dependency and rationality in his *Dependent Rational Animals: Why Human Beings Need the Virtues* (Chicago: Open Court, 1999).

20 MacIntyre, "Catholic Universities," 15.

21 MacIntyre, "Catholic Universities," 15–16.

Preface

1   Luigi Giussani, *Realtà e giovinezza: La sfida* [Reality and Youth: The Challenge] (Milan: Rizzoli, 2018), 209.

2   Giacomo Leopardi, "Imitazione" [Imitation], v. 3, *Cara Beltà...* (Milan: BUR, 2002), 113.

3   Elio Toaff and Alain Elkann, *Essere ebreo* [Being a Jew] (Milan: Bompiani, 1994), 40. Translation ours.

4   Romano Guardini, *L'essenza del Cristianesimo* [The Essence of Christianity] (Brescia: Morcelliana, 1981), 12. Translation ours.

5   Gal 2:20.

6   This is a reference to a debate that took place during a series of talks on "Freedom and value" (*Libertà e valore*), which were held at the Centro Culturale San Fedele (San Fedele Cultural Centre) in Milan on 12 and 13 March 1959.

7   Thomas Aquinas, *Summa Theologiae*, I, q. 16, article 1.

8   Giacomo Leopardi, "To His Lady," v. 12–22, 45–55, in *Canti*, translated and annotated by Jonathan Galassi (New York: Farrar, Straus and Giroux, 2010), 145–7

9   Jn 1:14.

10 Giulio Augusto Levi, *Giacomo Leopardi* (Messina: Principato, 1931).

11 See the *Letter to Diognetus*, paragraph 5, in *Patrologia Graeca*, ed. J.P. Migne, vol. 2 (Paris: 1857–86), 1167–86.

12 See Franz Kafka, *The Blue Octavo Notebooks* (Cambridge, MA: Exact Change, 1991).

13 This is a reference to the conference "Uomini e Religioni" [Men and Religions], held in Milan from 19 to 11 September 1993.

14 See Jn 14:6.

15 Heinrich Schlier, *Linee fondamentali di una teologia paolina* [Basic Elements of Pauline Theology] (Brescia: Queriniana, 1985), 119. Translation ours.

16 Mt 28:20.

17 1 Pt 1:25.

Introductory Thoughts

1 See Augustine, *Sermons on Selected Lessons of the New Testament*, XLVIII, 1 (Aeterna Press 2016). Online edition.

2 Hans Urs von Balthasar, *The Glory of the Lord: A Theological Aesthetics*, trans. Erasmo Leiva-Merikakis, ed. Joseph Fessio, S.J., and John Riches, vol. I: *Seeing the Form* (San Francisco: Ignatius Press, 1982), 183.

3 Gn 1:26.

4 Is 55:7–9.

5 Lk 17:10.

6 Jn 17:1.

7 Thomas Aquinas, *Summa Theologiae*, III, q. 8, art. 4.

8 "Ubi caritas et amor," in *Canti* (Milan: Coop. Edit. Nuovo Mondo, 2002), 69.

9 Mi 6:8.

10 Here see page 43.

11 Here see page 66–7.

12 Luigi Giussani, "Dio ha bisogno degli uomini," [God needs people] in *Il libro del Meeting '85: La Bestia, Parsifal e Superman* [The book of the Rimini Meeting 1985: The Beast, Percival, and Superman], ed. E. Neri, 175. Paper presented at the *Meeting per l'amicizia tra i popoli*, August 1985. Translation ours.

Chapter One

1 J.A. Jungmann, S.J., *Christus als Mittelpunkt religiöser Erziehung* (Freiburg: Herder, 1939), 20. Translation ours.

2 See C.G. Jung, *Modern Man in Search of a Soul* (New York: Routledge, 2001).

3 G. Gamaleri, "Una scuola di 'spostati'" [A school of "troublemakers"], in *Milano Studenti*, no. 2 (February–March 1960): 13.

4 Jn 1:10 (Vulgate).

5 Eph 4:15 (Vulgate).

6 Thomas Aquinas, *Quaestiones Disputatae de Veritate*, q. 10, art. 8, pt. c.

7 Eugenio Montale, "Forse un mattino andando in un'aria di vetro…" [Maybe one morning going along in the glassy air…] from *Ossi di seppia* [Cuttlefish Bones] in *Tutte le Poesie* [Collected Poems] (Milano: Oscar Mondadori, 1990), 42. Translation ours.

8 Gamaleri, "Una scuola," 13.

9 Seneca, *Epistles*, trans. Richard Mott Gummere, vol. 3 (Epistles 93–124), letter 108, "On the approaches to philosophy," pt. 23 (Cambridge: Harvard University Press, 1925).

10 Pope Pius XII, Encyclical Letter, *Fidei Donum*, Vatican website (21 April 1957), section II, 238. http://w2. vatican.va/content/pius-xii/it/encyclicals/documents/ hf_p-xii_enc_21041957_fidei-donum.html. The original line, which does not appear in the English translation of the Encyclical, reads: "*Le prospettive universali della Chiesa saranno le prospettive normali della sua vita cristiana.*"

11 Jn 8:34.

12 Cesare Balbo, *Le speranze d'Italia* (Turin: UTET, 1925), 272. Translation ours.

13 Mt 23:10 (Vulgate).

Chapter Two

1 See Augustine, *De peccatorum meritis et remissione et de baptism paruulmum*, II, 19, 32.

2 See Mt 19:28–9; Mk 10:28–30.

3 Jn 3:9.

4 Mt 9:16 (Vulgate).